the Son Rises

Resurrecting the Resurrection

ROBERT L. WISE

Regal

From Gospel Light
Ventura, California, U.S.A.

Published by Regal
From Gospel Light
Ventura, California, U.S.A.
www.regalbooks.com
Printed in the U.S.A.

Library of Congress Cataloging-in-Publication Data
Wise, Robert L.
The Son rises : resurrecting the resurrection / Robert L. Wise.
p. cm.
ISBN 978-0-8307-4569-2 (hard cover) — ISBN 978-0-8307-4621-7 (international
trade paper)
1. Jesus Christ—Resurrection. I. Title.
BT482.W58 2008
232'.5—dc22
2007034015

1 2 3 4 5 6 7 8 9 10 / 10 09 08 07

Rights for publishing this book outside the U.S.A. or in non-English languages are
administered by Gospel Light Worldwide, an international not-for-profit ministry.
For additional information, please visit www.glww.org, email info@glww.org, or write
to Gospel Light Worldwide, 1957 Eastman Avenue, Ventura, CA 93003, U.S.A.

Contents

Part Four: The Discovery

Acknowledgments

I send my deepest appreciation to the people who shared their stories of faith and personal discovery with me. Within these pages are the factual stories as they happened. In a few incidences names were changed to protect individuals, but the stories are true and occurred in the manner described.

Bernice McShane and Marketta Kelly always provide the proofreading that only dear friends can offer. Alex Field and the staff at Regal Books have been excellent. And thanks to Greg Johnson, my faithful and good agent.

The Situation
A.D. 33

"Good heavens!" Miriam looked up at her son rushing through the door. "Can't you walk into our house like a normal person? You were supposed to return hours ago."

"But . . ." Daniel gasped for air. "I-I must tell you what I have s-seen."

"Your mother's right," Abram demanded. "Don't come rushing in here."

Daniel leaned over their small table and tried to catch his breath. "Please, father. I am sorry but you must listen to me." Daniel caught another gulp of air. "I ran all the way."

"Supper has already been served," Miriam argued. "We're eating."

Daniel held up his hand. "I know that you did not believe Jesus of Nazareth was the Messiah," Daniel began slowly, "but . . ."

Abram nodded. "The man was crucified. What more is there to be said?"

"Yes, that's true. But I just came back from Galilee where 500 people saw Him."

"Who?" Maria shrugged.

"Jesus!" Daniel exploded. "Jesus of Nazareth!"

Abram's eyes widened. "What?"

"A few people in the crowd were there on the day of the crucifixion and saw the horror of His death, but there He was standing before us! Alive!"

Miriam's frown darkened. "Is this some joke?"

"No! I saw Him, I tell you! Jesus looked into my eyes as if He had already seen my doubts and was able to read my reservations . . . and He still smiled."

Miriam's frown turned into a look of dismay.

"Jesus held up His hand in blessing. The sleeve fell back and I could see His wrist where the spike had been driven through. Jesus said to us, 'The wounds frighten you, but be not afraid. Pain is redeemed by pain. Do not judge the future by the past. Expect redemption and it shall be yours.'"

Anger drained from Miriam's eyes and only astonishment remained.

"I know Jesus of Nazareth lives, and I'm going to follow Him," Daniel said.

Abram looked at Miriam and then back at Daniel. "Son, how can you follow a man who has already been crucified?"

"Because I saw Him with my own two eyes! He is *alive*, resurrected from the dead—and He promised He would be with us always."

When the Son Comes Up!

Let's go back to A.D. 33.

There were no churches, no evangelists on the street corner, no television preachers and no benevolence organizations. It was an age without radio or the Internet. Airplanes weren't even a dream and the only source of energy to propel a ship was slave power. It could take months for horses to carry a message over the mountains. The only means of spreading the word about anything was "tell-a-person," a means not as effective as it might seem. If the leader of a new cause was killed, that was the end of the movement.

Mystery cults abounded, dedicated to the likes of Dionysus, Artemis of the Ephesians or the river-god Meander. Each sect had its own bizarre rituals. Take the Taurobolium, an initiation ceremony for devotees of the goddess Cybele, for instance. In this magical little number, a bull was driven up a ramp under which people could walk. After being tied in place, the animal's throat was cut. As the blood poured down, new members of the sect walked underneath and were drenched in a downpour of liquid crimson.

The world of Jesus' time was scientifically and technologically light-years behind our own, and when Jesus died on the cross, the entire business He proclaimed should have died with

Him. Yet within 35 years of His death, so many believers lived in Rome that Nero could blame the Christians for burning the entire city. In a scant 300 years, the entire Roman Empire turned from politics to religion in an attempt to reunify the state. Christianity became the most powerful religion in the ancient world.

How could the death of a teacher in an obscure region, who was beaten to a pulp and then hung on a tree to die, turn into a force that overtook the world?

Only one explanation has stood the test of 2,000 years: Jesus Christ was resurrected from the dead.

What They Saw

In all of history, there remains only a handful of eyewitness accounts of the life and death of Jesus of Nazareth, which we have collected in one book, the Bible. In the New Testament, we are offered four perspectives from four different authors: Matthew, Mark, Luke and John. Told from decidedly different viewpoints, the overarching story is that a carpenter-turned-spiritual teacher named Jesus was sold out by one of His followers and, after a highly questionable trial conducted by the Jews and Romans, sentenced to death.

As was the custom of the Romans, Jesus went through a humiliating flogging, was driven down the streets of Jerusalem carrying a cross and was taken outside the city gates to be executed. After being impaled on that cross, He did nothing to save His own life, but hung there until He breathed His last and it was finished. Because His death occurred on the Friday evening of the Great Sabbath associated with Passover, He was hurriedly buried in a borrowed tomb near the sight of the execution. With terrified haste, His followers sealed the tomb and scattered. The entire scenario appeared to be an ignominious ending to a glorious three years of teaching, preaching and ministering. There wasn't much more to be said.

Except—

When some of the women who followed Jesus returned to the tomb three days later, He was gone! One account says that an angelic being told them Jesus had risen from His grave (see Mark 16:1-6). Later, more than 500 people saw Him at one time (see 1 Cor. 15:6)! There is no other reasonable explanation for how a dead man's teaching became a worldwide force except that something miraculous, powerful and transcendent did indeed occur.

The entire event was surrounded by mystery and seemed to defy logic. The elusiveness of the resurrection appearances followed a design known only to heaven. And those who saw Him were left in awe and uncertainty about what would happen next.

To get a better understanding of what happened and of the magnitude of the results of the resurrection, let's go back and take a hard look.

How They Were Changed

As Old Testament history unfolds, we see that the Jews developed ideas and doctrines about resurrection, but that these notions were generally in an apocalyptic context. The Sadducees and Samaritans, different religious and ethnic sects within first-century Judaism, rejected the idea entirely. Most of Jesus' followers (if not all), therefore, were unprepared for what was to come.

The Gospels make it clear that His death sent them running. Far from heroes, on the day of the resurrection they were still hiding like cowards, lest they too end up on crosses. Only Jesus' appearances after His resurrection nullified their fears.

The astonishing thing is that Jesus clearly announced His death and resurrection before they took place. In Mark's Gospel, we learn that before the Transfiguration, Jesus "began to teach them that the Son of Man must suffer many things and be rejected . . . and that he must be killed and after three days rise again" (Mark 8:31, *NIV*). Peter rebuked Jesus for expressing such an absurd idea, but Jesus rebuked His disciple right back (see Mark 8:32-33). Long before He arrived in Jerusalem, He laid it all on the table.

Jesus Himself taught His own return from the dead, and that's exactly what the New Testament records. Two thousand years after the resurrection, we still struggle to explain what occurred. Jesus' returning bodily from the dead defies medical or natural explanations for how a corpse could recover life. Mystery surrounds the empty tomb and theologians quarrel over its meaning. We are forced to either accept or reject that it really happened.

For 40 days after that first Easter morning, resurrection appearances continued in surprising and unexpected forms. The early believers could say with the Apostles, "We have seen the Lord!" The endurance and vitality of their experiences propelled them beyond locked doors, and as their testimonies spread, the resurrection of Jesus gripped imaginations across the ancient world. Its endurance throughout the centuries, however, had to be of more substance than a good story that

Two thousand years after

the resurrection, we still struggle

to explain what occurred.

Mystery surrounds the empty tomb

and theologians quarrel over

its meaning. We are forced to

either accept or reject that

it really happened.

tickled people's hopes. That Jesus' resurrection was real and transformed lives can be seen in the first Christians, who chose persecution and death rather than repudiate the story to avoid torture and the threat of execution. Facing harassment from the Roman Empire, they persevered regardless of the cost.

And it didn't stop with the end of the first century. Christian history contains abundant evidence that encounters with the Risen Lord have continued down the ages.

It is this kind of encounter that we need today.

A New World?

The first Christians saw the resurrection of Jesus Christ as the start of a new age, like the freshness of spring breaking through after a long and terrible winter. For them, an entirely new era had dawned, when death no longer needed to be feared. The cross of Jesus Christ had driven a stake through the Evil One. No longer would the specter of death be a sickle ready to wipe away humanity. The new credo of the Christian community declared that life reaches beyond the grave into an eternal tomorrow.

In contrast, on January 1, 2000, the hands of the clock passed midnight and a new millennium burst forth—without the expected Y2K disaster. Computers didn't explode, electricity continued and the television kept playing. Nothing stopped. The planet kept rocking along on its way to who knows where. Few (if any) would say that a new era emerged, transforming people's lives in undeniable and irrevocable ways.

A survey by the Barna Group attempted to pinpoint American values. Their poll described a list of 17 activities, and responders indicated what they liked to do best. Seventy-one percent (7 out of 10) put "getting a good night of sleep" at the top of their wish list, while only 40 percent wanted to go to church. A good mattress beat out the venerable pulpit! Listening to music (54 percent) and being with friends (55 percent) also ranked higher than church.[1]

Our "new world" looks an awful lot like the old one.

The *Nothing* in Traditional Church

Why are we stuck in the pursuit of ease, comfort and the good life? Have 2,000 years of history produced little more than the same old quest for indulgence, affluence and self-promotion? Why are we not flocking into churches to hear the story of this amazing resurrection?

Powerful preaching and meaningful worship appear to be parked out back in the car lot. The Church doesn't seem to know what to do with the resurrection story beyond recite that it happened an awfully long time ago. Why in the world would this amazing account be pushed into the corner of dim recollection? Let's take a look at the expectations we might be bringing with us to church. What's really going on?

Take Harold and Harriet Jones for example. Nice, middle-class Americans in their mid-60s, they both grew up in neighborhood churches. Ask Harold about his expectations for Sunday morning worship down at the little white building with the steeple on the top. What does Harold anticipate will happen on Sunday morning? How about Harriet? Given their experience, the Joneses expect something like this during their average worship service:

The greeter at the door is the guy who's been shaking hands for the last 50 years. The Joneses sit in the same pew they've occupied for a decade and wait for the pastor to come in a side door and sit down on the big stuffed chair in the middle of the elevated platform, grinning a welcome to Harold and Harriet. Soft music in the background covers the sound of the choir shuffling in, dressed in robes the same color they've been since the Vietnam War. Once everybody's seated, the pastor starts the ball rolling with Scripture and a long prayer. The sermon always goes on and on and gives the Joneses some insight in how to live better. (Mainly the pastor tells them to shape up.) On this Sunday, the message is a scolding for the legislation allowing gambling that voters just passed.

Everything ends with another somber prayer, and then people noisily file out on their way to a cup of coffee in the basement. Harold and Harriet greet a few friends and comment that the audience seems to be smaller than it once was.

Every week is predictable and not much changes until they get to Christmas and Easter. In between the high seasons, the pulse of worship is as even as the pavement on the parking lot. Most members haven't heard powerful preaching in so long that they wouldn't recognize it if it bit them on the nose.

What happened to Harold and Harriet Jones in church? Nothing. Absolutely nothing. Sadly, this *nothing* has become the main problem with many American churches.

The *Emptiness* of Alternative Churches

Harold and Harriet would certainly be shocked if they hit one of the up-and-coming mega-churches with the dance band, huge screens hanging from rafters and trendy music accompanying the periodic drama skits. These larger-than-life congregations of

20- to 45-year olds are as new as the millennium and filled with sparkles and surprises. Rather than the pastor ambling in from a side door, worship starts with a broadcast from the screens blaring advertisements for coming events. Far from the unsurprising services the Joneses attend, *unpredictability* is the key word.

As members file in with coffee cups in hand or holding doughnuts to eat during worship, people begin clapping and the show starts. Sometimes the lights lower to total darkness and then come up with a boom as a band cranks out the latest praise and worship music. When the preaching begins, the topics generally surprise and titillate the audience. (This wouldn't be what the Joneses had in mind either.)

No one can fault these forms of worship for attempting to be relevant by finding meaningful ways to engage the congregation. With innovations in music and approach, many of these mega-congregations are reaching the unchurched in new and vital ways. Can't be critical of that approach! So, what's the issue here?

The question is this: Is entertainment and sensory stimulation really an appropriate goal for worship? Are we on the right track when the competition is the movies? The mega-church alternative tends to reflect the financial goals of a success-driven middle-class crowd far more than it echoes a biblical and spiritual quest. Many of these institutions have mistaken emotion for inspiration and relevance for revelation.

When it's all boiled down, the flash and flare cover a profound emptiness. Harold and Harriet Jones wouldn't understand why they were more bothered than attracted to one of these "hot" churches, but in the end they might sense that after

Both the old and the new congregations sit on a featureless planet where no one has seen God in a long, long time. The problem is that we are trying to substitute a "song and dance" routine to keep members coming while waiting for the real Source of vitality to show up (and no one's got a clue when that will be).

the noise died out and the television screens were turned off, there actually wasn't anything going on! Both the old and the new congregations sit on a featureless planet where no one has seen God in a long, long time. The problem is that we are trying to substitute a "song and dance" routine to keep members coming while waiting for the real Source of vitality to show up (and no one's got a clue when that will be).

The shared dilemma is that both the staid traditional church and the hyped-up contemporary church fundamentally reflect American society. While their styles differ radically, the direction of these churches is governed by a capitalist society that salutes the Constitution and charges off after success at almost any cost. The goal is to reflect society's prevailing current norms. We lose our way when we forget that Church isn't about adapting to society or accommodating culture. Christian worship comes from a source completely foreign to our society. It is called the resurrection of Jesus Christ.

The Plunge into Pluralism

Once upon a time, your seventh-grade teacher started her American history lesson by telling the class that they lived in a Christian nation. Today, she would be fired for such a comment. Things have changed.

Over the last 50 years, American society has radically shifted in its religious interest. Most people have little or no concern for what happens in a church on Sunday morning. Contemporary television has seduced society into spending Sunday morning getting ready to watch professional football or basketball games, or whatever else is being played out on the large screen in the living room. The focus is now on a beer, a bowl of popcorn and the Bears, the Buccaneers or the Bulls.

During the past five decades, politicians, sociologists and historical theorists have decreed that we misread the founders of the country and the signers of the Declaration of Independence. We've been told most of the originators weren't Christian and never envisioned a Christian society: Their goal and design was pluralism, in which all religions have equal footing. In this shift from a Christian orientation to an "it's all good" persuasion, Christian denominations that once dominated national life have experienced a frightening departure of their membership. Mainliners have turned into sideliners.

The question about what happened on Easter morning is no longer asked. The tenets of the faith have disappeared and culturally acceptable substitutes have slipped in. The creeds of Christendom that were created to proclaim an unchangeable faith have been redefined as mere "road signs" that pointed to our present, when faith has to adapt and change to make people feel more comfortable. In many instances, pastors construct their own doctrines and approaches that differ significantly from the roots of apostolic faith. If the changes seem strange and out of order, congregations throw in a few guitars, a set of drums and sing more enthusiastically. Extra emotion might drown out dissent.

The Church has experienced serious and dangerous fragmentation. Biblical faith has been pushed aside for social activism. There is no longer anyone in the driver's seat and the car is flying off the road. The ancient faith that came down to us from antiquity has become suspect, and we are told that we cannot look to the past for direction. We must allow the unfolding social scene to show us what to do next. Fragmentation has left the American church open to serious misdirection and misinterpretation of the faith. Pastors stand up and preach from this posture to bewildered congregations. When Harold and Harriet Jones hear messages that arise from this mentality, they find themselves confused and uncertain. After enough of this confusion, they quit going to worship. The promise of the new millennium seems to be in technology, with not much coming from church. What can the Joneses do?

Resurrecting the Resurrection

As important as the quest for relevance is, it must not be the bottom line for the Church. Across the centuries there have been many changes and new paths that have emerged, but the driving force behind the Church at its best and most effective has never been humor, cleverness or trendiness. Show business has never shown the Church off to an advantage. Rather, the essence of the Christian faith profoundly touching the soul of the listeners is what has sustained and transformed the community of believers.

In the past the gospel was preached with a reality that listeners could encounter. Believers discovered the opportunity to have personal and intimate communication with God, just as Jesus promised they would. The blessings and interventions of the Holy Spirit released vitality that sent people on their way rejoicing because they had found a new capacity to endure whatever life had in store for them. Rather than simply being enthused, they were empowered. What was it that made such a difference? *The story of the resurrection of Jesus Christ from the dead set believers free to become new people!*

The need of *this* hour is to resurrect the resurrection.

Our pressing urgency is to meet the risen Christ just as the first Apostles did and to hear His voice offering direction. This resurrected Lord stood before His followers and promised them, "I am with you always, to the very end of the age" (Matt. 28:20, *NIV*).

The "always" Jesus promised extended beyond the first century and continues into this new millennium and beyond, to this very hour.

An Encounter with the Risen Christ

While developing this book, I documented the stories of people who have had spiritual encounters with Jesus Christ. With tape recorder in hand, I asked for a candid report of how they had experienced Him in their lives. The range of stories was wide and varying, but they all aligned with what the New Testament says can be expected. I found their accounts to be inspiring and transforming, as well as suggestive of a new path for our time. These supernatural encounters happen with greater frequency than people realize. They are often so overwhelming that the individual doesn't talk about his or her experience, so the wider Body of Christ rarely learns of it—to our detriment.

With her three children, Donna Rowland moved into a duplex next door to her parents in Denver, Colorado. Unfortunately, her mother and father had an overwhelming drinking problem that turned Donna's world upside down. With her parent's alcoholism spiraling downward, she fought depression and wasn't sure where to turn. In 1972 at age 28, Donna should have been in the prime of her life. Sadly, she was in the dumps and no one offered any significant help.

Finally, Donna called a friend who had always been sensitive and helpful. She was the only person to suggest that Donna needed divine guidance. The idea connected. Donna wondered why no one else had offered such advice. However, Donna quickly recognized a problem. Even though she knew the thought was wrong, the truth was that she loved her three children more than she loved God. Donna confessed this wasn't right, but it was the truth. Her friend had a response. Why not talk to God and tell Him how she felt? She could tell God that she was giving the children to Him and that would end the matter. Donna agreed that she would do this.

When she got off the phone, Donna walked into her kitchen, leaned against the cabinets, and prayed. "God, I give You my children. I desperately need Your intervention and I want to put You in Your rightful place."

Donna waited, not knowing what to expect—but nothing happened. For a few moments, she even wondered if there was a God. Her despondency deepened and she decided to go to bed. Sitting down on the edge of the mattress, she prayed one last time. "God, if You are for real, You can come down here and sit on the edge of the bed and get this problem straightened out for me. If not, well . . ."

Donna pulled back the covers and got into bed. With nothing but blackness before her, she rolled over and went to sleep. In the middle of the night, she woke up. Getting out of bed, Donna strolled into the backyard. The June summer night had a pleasant warmth to it. As Donna looked up, to her shock, Jesus Christ was standing before her dressed in a white robe. The risen Christ looked at Donna with deep compassion and extended His hands. Automatically, she reached for Him and they began to communicate telepathically. Donna could sense His deepest feelings and realized how profoundly Christ loved her. His love for the whole world settled over her with a peace that was beyond all understanding. To her total surprise, Donna realized that Jesus had the maturity of an adult, and yet the innocence of a child.

The experience was so overwhelming that Donna no longer wanted to return to her three children. She was ready to stay with the risen Christ forever, but Donna knew that this wasn't possible—she had to go on with her life. With the greatest reluctance, she turned around toward her house.

The next thing Donna knew was that she was back in her bed. She sat up with a jolt and realized this had actually happened in her sleep, but it was the most real experience of her life. Donna fell back on her pillow with the reality of the encounter covering her like a warm blanket. For the next two days, Donna had a corner in her house where she would go and sit to remember how much Jesus Christ loved her. Even as she told me her story, tears still filled her eyes.

In the days and weeks that followed, Donna developed an intense hunger for the Bible. She started going to church again.

The need of this hour is to resurrect the resurrection. Our pressing urgency is to meet the risen Christ just as the first Apostles did and to hear His voice offering direction. This resurrected Lord stood before His followers and promised them, "I am with you always, to the very end of the age."

Yet one of the most startling aspects of this experience came in the next few days. As she drove down the street, the grass appeared greener and the sky bluer. Everything looked new because Donna was new. Her relationship with men changed. Because her problems with her father had been so severe, Donna had developed a tendency to shy away from her husband's male friends. After this personal discovery of Jesus Christ, she enjoyed people as never before. Her perspective had changed.

Donna had no idea why such a marvelous breakthrough had come in her life—she could only attribute it to the grace of divine love. From her few moments with the Person of the risen Christ, she learned that when we are insufficient, He is all-sufficient. Donna had truly entered a new world.

In the following chapters, we will examine the resurrection and explore its meaning. You will have the opportunity to discover the risen Christ, who is ready to touch your life, to walk with you, to talk with you and to give you entry into eternity. It may prove to be the most important discovery of your life.

Note

1. The Barna Group, "Americans Just Want a Good Night of Sleep," released on October 16, 2006. http://www.barna.org/FlexPage.aspx?Page=BarnaUpdate&BarnaUpdateID=247 (accessed November 2007).

How Did We Get Here?

If the event of the Son's rising is so critical, why is the story told to the Sunday morning congregation with little more zeal than sharing what one had for breakfast? Why has the resurrection been reduced to a vague memory, a recollection, a far distant event? If on Easter morning, someone stood up in the church Harold and Harriet Jones attend to relate that earlier in the morning they had "seen the Lord," the congregation would explode with outrage—no one considers this to be a contemporary event.

I tried to confront this problem several decades ago. Recognizing that the congregation I pastored saw Easter as little more than an opportunity to buy a new dress, have ham for Sunday lunch and pick spring daffodils, I decided to shake people up. I began that morning's sermon with a rambling, boring account of where the custom of Easter eggs originated—I had arranged for a friend to come in the back door five minutes into my message and shout that the service had to stop. Sure enough, the double doors flew open and John Cruetier came running down the aisle in Bermuda shorts, tennis shoes and a dirty shirt.

"I saw it on television!" John shouted and waved his arms in the air. "I was doing my yard work because it's such a beautiful spring day. I came in the house for a drink and there it was on TV."

"What, John?" I said from the pulpit. "What are you talking about? Why are you interrupting the service?"

"The television said that in New York City a man had seen Jesus alive!" John shouted. "Truly alive! And a lady in Los Angeles had the same experience! They are saying that Jesus is as alive as you sit here in these pews."

The results of my attempt at innovation? Not particularly positive. About half the congregation thought John had been drinking, and most of the rest thought I'd pulled the stunt to keep them awake through the end of the sermon (they were closer to the truth). Almost no one got the point that the experiment was an attempt to awaken them to the conviction that Jesus of Nazareth is alive, and that they could encounter Him as the disciples did, as recorded in the New Testament. Despite my best efforts, the Son didn't come up on that Easter morning.

Why did this group of people refuse to entertain the notion that the resurrection was actually a possibility? What had created a good congregation of fine people who accepted the miraculous underpinning of their faith as no more than an excuse to chat and drink coffee in the fellowship hall following the service? As the years went on, I was intrigued and dismayed to realize that this congregation was not unique but the norm in the American scene.

Who dropped the ball?

Pedestrian Preoccupation

The loss of a personal discovery of the resurrected Christ is not a new epidemic. In recent decades, as the shape of American life has changed, the shift has become more profound, but the loss of individual contact with the Christ is an old, old affliction that goes back to the first century. The sickness breaks out again and again.

As evolutionists enjoy pointing out, life is a battle for survival and only the toughest endure the constant struggle. Even though we've put away the spears, swords and axes, we have replaced them with pistols, bombs and horrific weapons of mass destruction. Our attempts not to drown in the muck of human existence cause us to keep our eyes on the ground, and watching the path in front of us doesn't give us much time to look to the heavens. Preoccupation with daily life—cutting the grain, grinding the wheat, making the bread (or simply running down to the grocery store)—pushes aside the spiritual dimension of human existence. Whether on the battlefield or on a city street, we lose Jesus in the roaring threat of destruction or the roaring of the subway train.

While the movies portray violent assaults by vicious criminals charging through front doors with weapons drawn, the real enemy of American Christians is a product of affluence. We are the children of plenty, and unfortunately, the result is not satisfaction but a desire for more. Our lives turn into a recycled routine of going to bed at a certain hour, getting up to an alarm clock, going to work at exactly the same time, taking vacations at the prescribed time each year—on and on. This repeating half-life of making and spending money is pretty much where middle-class America lives.

During World War II, Dietrich Bonhoeffer wrote that affluence produces apathy. His insight was that a great many of us never encounter a spiritual breakthrough because we don't care enough to go out looking for one. Wealth (or enough money that we appear to be wealthy to people just beneath us) creates an insulation that makes it nearly impossible for the intangible and eternal to penetrate. Bonhoeffer understood that ease produces a dullness of mind and spirit that tends to kill the quest for the highest and best.[1]

People with affluence, position and power are also apt to use their opportunities for themselves, rather than seeking the higher way. In 2007, America debated whether the many marriages and affairs of Rudy Giuliani and Newt Gingrich made them poor candidates for the U.S. presidency—and into the mix was dredged up Bill Clinton, Gennifer Flowers and Monica Lewinski in the 1990s. Where has this disregard for marital fidelity come from? Like apathy, lust can be helped along by prosperity.

Is this news? It certainly shouldn't be.

In a society of substance, what can break the indifference pattern? Unfortunately, personal tragedy can be depended on to shatter the illusion that we are self-sufficient. Unexpected emotional upheaval turns the car over—we look around as we climb through the broken windows and discover that the world is different from what we thought it was. A precipitous drop in the stock market, the death of a spouse, the loss of a child, a career failure . . . the disruption of the pattern of plenty that we believed was permanent often begins our search in a new direction.

No one takes joy in such disruption and most of us would do anything to avoid it. Yet preoccupation with pedestrian matters—just striving to survive from morning to night—has blinded so many of us from knowing the personal breakthrough and spiritual discovery of the risen Christ. And many who experience devastating calamity look back from the far side of disaster and are thankful for it.

Unbalanced Theology

Another contributing factor to our loss of a profound resurrection experience is partial or confused theology. What do we hear preached on Sunday? What's the content of the messages we receive week after week?

While the average churchgoer doesn't necessarily think in these terms, it is important to realize that every pastor is a reflection of a theological system that he or she learned in seminary or picked up along the way. There is a message behind the message. For example, for decades the average church majored in evangelism. The "hidden message" was an emphasis on conversion that was focused on what you *believed*. In the late '60s and into the '70s, the emphasis shifted—the backdrop became social action. Each sermon was crafted to get listeners to do something about a social condition in society. War, poverty, civil rights and so on became the unspoken implication of every homily. The issue wasn't what you believed, but rather what you *did*.

Today, a large section of the American Church is concerned about what you *feel*. Leaving worship feeling good has become important, because good feelings are a major goal for an affluent society. In this sense, the modern worship movement has tended to swallow the historicity of the Christian story. The pep band, endless singing of one-line ditties, flashing lights, media screens—the whole show—are aimed at creating an

Christianity is grounded in history, not sensation. The earliest believers followed Jesus Christ not because it felt good, but because they discovered the Son's rising was the only reality that could be counted on in a world of constant change.

emotional juggernaut that bowls people over and sends them home on a high. We assume that the powerful emotions we have experienced equate with experiencing Christ, but if that's true, a football or basketball game is just as spiritually effective as church.

When the focal point of the Christian journey is off-center, personal quest becomes skewed and misses the target. I once sat on a hillside in San Francisco and watched ocean freighters leaving the harbor to make their way across the Pacific Ocean. It occurred to me that a ship's captain could be only a few degrees off when plotting his course for Hawaii, and it wouldn't mean a thing getting out of the harbor. But by the time he should have reached Honolulu, those few degrees would have put him on his way to Japan.

There are not many churches today holding seminars or workshops directing people in how they can encounter the risen Christ. The loss of this compass of the Christian faith has turned us into ships that flow wherever the tide of emotion takes us. But Christianity is grounded in history, not sensation. The earliest believers followed Jesus Christ not because it felt good, but because they discovered the Son's rising was the only reality that could be counted on in a world of constant change.

Reason vs. Experience

In addition to affluent preoccupation and poor theology, we might consider how the impact of the Enlightenment, which gained a foothold in the late seventeenth and early eighteenth centuries, turned faith into an intellectual quest and a sword

35

fight between differing ideologies. The test of truth became rationalism and reason became supreme. From this logic-bias came Deism (the idea that God is absent and the world runs by natural law, like a clock ticking), which still rules in many denominations today. Most church members don't recognize that they live in this intellectually slanted world, but they have nonetheless been highly impacted by its consequences. They worry when personal experience doesn't fit with what seems rational. Experiencing the risen Christ? Too unreasonable.

At the other extreme, we might consider the many Christians who seek to be as "far out" as possible and distrust any form of objective analysis. Religion is a "trip" for them. They fail to see how an encounter with Jesus Christ must impact their daily behavior and change their lives. We see the influence of these "Christian thrill-seekers" in the profound lack of drastically changed lives within the Church.

Few people know how to approach the blurry line between abstract experience and what is generally accepted as scientific and reasonable. And when we are unwilling to deal with the seeming gap between the natural and the supernatural, encounters with the risen Christ slip away into the DO NOT TOUCH bin. The disconcerting is left unexamined because of our preference for comfort.

An Encounter with the Risen Christ

George Lewis checked into Sky Ridge Medical Center because surgery appeared inevitable. With an excellent physician, every conceivable test had been run and the results supported the doctor's diagnosis: George was in trouble. However, he was a devout man who prayed. On Tuesday afternoon, the pastor from George's church dropped by to make sure he was spiritually prepared for what he was about to face.

"You look good," Pastor Kendricks said thoughtfully.

"You won't believe how good I feel," George said. "Pastor, I had the most amazing dream."

"Oh! Tell me about it."

George became thoughtful. "I slipped off into a nap just a bit ago. Guess I was more weary than I realized. As I was dreaming, I looked up and there at the foot of the bed stood Jesus. Standing there just like in the Bible, with an outer robe on."

The pastor's eyes widened. "That is quite a dream!"

"But it was so real. Life-like. The Lord Jesus smiled at me and a radiant love filled the room. And then Jesus opened the outer robe and underneath was a cure for every illness in the world. He came around the side of the bed and wrapped His robe around me. His hug was the most wonderful experience of my life."

The pastor blinked several times and stared. "I-I don't know what to say."

"Well, I can't tell you how good this dream left me feeling. It was like the risen Christ was truly here. Just amazing."

After the pastor prayed and left, the doctor came in and told George that even though they had run every possible test, he wanted to run a final check. After getting the results back, they'd start prepping him immediately for the operation.

In a couple of hours the doctor returned with a mystified look on his face. "I don't understand it, George, but the test didn't come back at all like I expected. The results indicate that you're normal and that can't be. We will be rerunning all the tests."

"Whatever you say, Doc," George said.

The doctor left and the testing began. To the astonishment of the entire hospital, every test came back with the same results: George Lewis was as normal as Monday morning. The physician cancelled the operation and George went home.

Any normal, logical thinking person would have to ask how such a thing could happen. The reversal of a string of medical tests because of a dream just doesn't occur. Until Jesus, the Risen One, gets involved.

It is stories like George's that convince me it's time to tear off the DO NOT TOUCH sign and move into the mystery beyond preoccupation, inadequate theology and insufficient rationalism: meeting the risen Christ.

Note

1. Dietrich Bonhoeffer, *The Cost of Discipleship* (New York: The MacMillian Co., 1963), pp. 105-201.

PART TWO

The Story
A.D. 33

*Now on the first day of the week Mary Magdalene
came early to the tomb, while it was still dark, and saw
the stone already taken away from the tomb.*

JOHN 20:1, *NASB*

Cleopas could not speak. His mouth opened, but no words came out. Pounding lightly on his chest, he took a deep breath.

"Did . . . did . . . we really see . . . *Him*?" his friend asked.

Night was settling in and the smell of food drifted in through the open window. Shadows had fallen over the inn. Unleavened bread left over from the Passover feast sat next to a clay cup. The simple cup stood in the center of the table, half-filled with wine. Two broken pieces of bread still lay on the earthen plate.

Cleopas rubbed his eyes and found it difficult to clear his throat. "He's gone! Gone right out of our sight!"

"But He was here. Wasn't He? I can't believe my own eyes."

"And we walked with Him all the way here. All the way to Emmaus! How did we fail to recognize who He was?"

"We were so sure He was dead," the friend said. "After all, Cleopas, we *saw* them take His body down and carry it away." Cleopas nodded as his friend continued, "I don't know what to make of it, but He is alive. Alive for sure!"

"No question about that," Cleopas said. "He talked to us like old friends, and shared the Scriptures beyond anything any other rabbi ever told us." He rubbed his beard. "There is no question it was Him."

"How can it be?"

"I don't know," Cleopas said, "but this I do understand: Jesus defeated death."

What Happened?

The question hidden in a mystery wrapped in an enigma is exactly what Mary Magdalene discovered on that first Easter morning. What happened between the time of Jesus' terrible death on Friday and the stone being rolled away on Sunday? Even firm believers in the resurrection don't agree on all the details, but everyone recognizes this as the bedrock issue.

James Cameron, director of the Oscar-winning movie *Titanic*, recently produced a documentary called *The Lost Tomb of Jesus*. The film's director, Simcha Jacobovici, and his crew claim to have discovered a limestone ossuary that, until 1980, contained the bones of Jesus. Laid in a family tomb that was uncovered during a construction project, one of the 10 boxes found in the tomb is alleged to have contained the bones of Jesus' son, Judah. Never mind that for 2,000 years no one ever heard of Jesus' having a son! (Even Anna Nicole Smith's baby got more publicity.) And who was Judah's mother? Why, Mary Magdalene of course! Is it a surprise after Dan Brown's novel *The Da Vinci Code* popularized the idea of a love affair between Jesus and Mary from Magdala that another of the ossuaries would be identified as hers? Needless to say, the story about the "Jesus Family's" lost tomb got considerable television coverage and more than a few headlines. (The filmmakers desperately hoped people would overlook the fact that the whole scenario sounds about as implausible as an American soap opera. And many people did.)

In the aftermath of the film, those who don't believe in the resurrection could rejoice and point to the story as evidence that they had been right all along. Believers, meanwhile, confidently forecasted the storm would blow over, pointing to scholars who have established that during the first century, the name *Jesus* was as common as *Smith* or *Jones*. The "evidence" for the tomb having been that of *the* Jesus is flimsy at best, and some would say the filmmakers made pieces fit that didn't belong to the same puzzle.

Apart from this side-show distraction, the real question that has continued throughout the ages is whether or not Jesus returned from the grave to walk the earth again. *What happened?*

Unraveling the Story

In order to get a firm grasp on what occurred, one must explore two things. First, what is the basic story? Like explaining the plot in a novel, we need to know all the details—who said what to whom, and so on. Our first task is to *lay out the storyline*.

Second, the story of Jesus' resurrection comes to us with a *theological perspective*. What is the religious meaning? How does the story fit into the plan of God? What does it tell us about the heavenly Father? What was the Creator's intention? By the second century, the Church had distilled the life of Jesus of Nazareth into creeds that framed Him within a broader theological scope. We must take a look at these creedal statements to understand how the earliest believers comprehended the resurrection as a part of God's plan for His creation.

Both of these perspectives provide a layer of the story, and we cannot get the full meaning of the resurrection without delving into each. To start our journey toward understanding, we will examine the possibilities in each and see what we discover. Eventually, we should be able to piece together a comprehensive picture of the facts and meaning of the resurrection of Jesus. We begin with the story itself.

Mark's Foundation

Probably the oldest of the four, the Gospel according to Mark tells a quick and sparse story in which the finale of the story was torn away—we can't be certain how the writer concluded.[1] Ancient Church Fathers such as Eusebius, Clement of Alexandria, Irenaeus and others indicated the Gospel was written in Rome for the Romans. Certainly, it seems to have been written for a non-Jewish readership. Because the apostle Peter (likely the eyewitness source for the Jesus stories) and Mark were together in Rome around A.D. 63, it has been suggested that the best date for the Gospel's writing is between A.D. 50 to 65. Because this period was a time of persecution, it is sometimes proposed that the ending of the Gospel could have been lost during a raid or assault on the first Christians.

It is significant to note that in 1972, Rev. Jose O'Callaghan, a Jesuit scholar at the University of Barcelona, published an argument that a fragment of Mark (7Q5) could be dated to A.D. 50. The fragment was found in cave number seven, with many of the other Dead Sea Scrolls. Father O'Callaghan held to the position that the entire book of Mark was likely written immediately after the crucifixion.[2]

While views differ, the totality of evidence builds a case for an extremely early record of the events surrounding the crucifixion and resurrection. Far from hearsay, the Gospel of Mark has all the hallmarks of an account by an eyewitness who described the details. While it is popular to suspect such accounts as spurious, it is important to note that these earliest witnesses to the resurrection died for their story. Their willing deaths certainly contribute to the validity of their reports—can we really believe they would knowingly die for a lie?

Mark's account tells us that three women went to the tomb very early on the first day of the week and found the stone rolled away (see Mark 16:1-8). One young man in a white robe told the women that Jesus was risen and had gone into Galilee where He would meet the disciples. The manuscript ends with the women leaving in fear. (Supplementary endings were added that reflect the beliefs of later times.)

Matthew's Account

A considerable number of scholars hold to the view that Matthew's Gospel came next in chronological order. It presents a thoroughly Jewish version of the crucifixion and resurrection story. We can surmise that Matthew's Gospel was probably written around A.D. 70 but no later—there is no mention of the devastating destruction of Jerusalem and the Temple, and it is hard to believe that such a catastrophic Jewish event would go

The earliest witnesses to the
resurrection died for their story.
Their willing deaths certainly
contribute to the validity
of their reports—can we really
believe they would knowingly
die for a lie?

unmentioned in an account written for a Jewish community.

Matthew tells us that two women found that an angel had moved the rock away from the tomb (see Matt. 28:1-15). This angel announced the resurrection and sent the women on their way with the promise of an appearance in Galilee. As they hurried away, Jesus Himself appeared to them and repeated the instruction to go to Galilee.

Interestingly, Matthew adds some details about the guards who were posted at the tomb. When they told the chief priests everything that had happened, the priests paid them to change their story—they were to say that the disciples had stolen the body while they were asleep. The illogic of this story seems to have escaped the chief priests: How could the guards know about the tomb robbery if they were sleeping?!

Matthew's Gospel ends with Jesus appearing in Galilee and declaring that all authority in heaven and on earth had been given to Him. The Apostles must go and make more disciples, baptizing them into fellowship with the Father, the Son and the Holy Spirit. Furthermore, Jesus would be with them to the end of the age (see Matt. 28:16-20).

Luke's Story

Written probably a decade after Matthew's, Luke's account adds details not recorded in the first two Gospels. A physician from Antioch in Syria, there is reason to believe that Luke eventually lived in Philippi. He was a convert from the Gentile world and was probably Greek. (In *Luke the Historian in the Light of Research*, first published in 1936, A. T. Robertson argues that Luke was a brother to Titus, which would have definitely made him Greek.[3])

Luke indicates that he is writing to give a clear and accurate account of what happened in the ministry of Jesus (see Luke 1:1-3) and the Early Church (see Acts 1:1-2). He is concerned with encouraging the faith of the believers as well as reaching all nations with the Good News of Jesus. Consequently, his Gospel tells us more and in greater detail than Mark about what Jesus did.

In his story of the resurrection, Luke adds another figure at the open tomb. He tells us that two men in "dazzling apparel" greeted the women (Luke 24:1 8, *ASV*). This account is followed by the story of Jesus' appearance on the road to Emmaus (see Luke 24:13-35). After talking with the resurrected Christ, Cleopas and his friend immediately returned to Jerusalem and told the Apostles what they had seen. As they were talking, Jesus suddenly appeared in the midst of them (see Luke 24:36-49).

Luke goes to considerable detail to make sure the reader understands that this was not a mystical appearance: Jesus showed His followers the wounds from the crucifixion and ate some fish to demonstrate that He was not a spirit. After Jesus had imparted understanding of the Scripture, He led them out to Bethany and ascended into heaven. The rest of Luke's story is told in the book of Acts.

Luke builds to the resurrection story, giving us a fuller and broader perspective of what occurred. There are some differences and we will consider these. In contrast to Matthew's Jewish emphasis, Luke writes to the Greek Theophilus (meaning "lover of God" in Greek) and speaks more directly to the world beyond the synagogue. We are left with a picture of the gospel moving quickly through countries surrounding Israel.

John's Word

The Gospel of John takes a startlingly different approach to the story of Jesus. The writer begins with an extraordinary description of Jesus the Christ as the *logos*, the Word of God, who came as the light to penetrate the darkness of all humanity. The power of this proclamation is an awesome presentation of Jesus Christ's identity in poetic and abstract terms.

Scholars differ on the identity of the writer, however. The current best estimate on the time of authorship suggests sometime between A.D. 90 and 100. Nearly a lifetime had passed since the writing of Mark's Gospel. Because of the great length of time between the crucifixion of Jesus and this Gospel's writing, there continues to be disagreement among biblical historians about whether or not the apostle John wrote it himself. Leaving all debates aside, the author turned his attention in a different philosophical direction from the other three Gospels, and the general consensus of the Church has been that John did indeed write it.

Each of the Gospels is different in purpose. Mark's story lays the facts on the table and implies that the reader must draw a conclusion. Matthew's account spells out the story for Jewish believers—focusing on Jesus' identity as the Messiah—while Luke aims at a Gentile mind. John takes an even more lofty perspective, framing the life of Jesus cosmically: Because Jesus is the *logos* of God, all believers can have eternal life through Him. John doesn't want the reader to go to bed and think about it overnight— he calls for a decision at the moment of reading.

His story also adds important details not found in the other Gospels. According to John, on Easter morning, Mary Magdalene found the tomb empty and ran to bring Simon Peter and another disciple, who investigated the scene and then left. Standing outside the tomb in distress, Mary encountered two angels and then the risen Lord, who told her that He had not yet ascended to His Father (see John 20:1-18).

As related in the other Gospels, Jesus appeared to the Apostles that evening, but John adds that Jesus breathed on them and told them to receive the Holy Spirit (see John 20:19-22). The apostle Thomas was not with them, and doubted their story, but eight days later, Doubting Thomas saw the resurrected Lord and touched the wounds of Christ (see John 20:24-29). His reservations vanished.

These stories reveal a hunger for more details on the part of the early believers. While John gave them more, his added stories are strangely mystical. Told in a matter of fact manner, they hint at the extraordinary and supernatural colliding with the ordinary and physical. For example, there is Mary's apparent difficulty recognizing Jesus (see John 20:14). The implication is that Jesus had significantly changed in some physical way that made it hard to identify Him when He appeared. At the same time, John is careful to make sure we know that His followers saw Jesus' physical presence, including the wounds in his hands and feet and his ability to eat. We are not hearing about a vision but are receiving an account of a solid, physical human who had the remarkable ability to appear and disappear. We are left with a need for more insight to grasp exactly what happened.

John adds an entirely new story about the Apostles going back to Galilee to their original vocation of fishing (see John 21). Jesus appeared and used the occasion to teach them about their new vocation—or to remind them that their original call was to be fishers of men! John ends his Gospel by telling readers that the world couldn't hold the books that might be written about everything that Jesus did. Certainly, John's Gospel adds an enlarged dimension to our insight.

So . . . What Is the Storyline?

A closer look at all four New Testament Gospels still leaves us confronted by the mystery within an enigma. The timeline, people and events recorded within each book are substantially different from one another, so much so that they exceed our ability to explain clearly. At the same time, these differences are what give the overarching storyline its mystery *and* believability. On the basis of nothing but the four resurrection stories, here are some conclusions I believe we can draw:

1. *The time gap between the crucifixion, the resurrection and the writing of the Gospels is so small as to be negligible.* Even if we take the maximum estimate for each book's date of writing, the accounts are within the lifetime of an eyewitness.

2. Whatever problems we have accepting the fact of resurrection, we should not worry that we are reading fictionalized accounts written long after what occurred. *The authenticity and reliability of the books of the New Testament have been firmly established.* We get a clearer picture of this reliability when we compare

The timeline, people and events recorded within each book are substantially different from one another, so much so that they exceed our ability to explain clearly. At the same time, these differences are what give the overarching storyline its mystery and believability.

the New Testament with other ancient documents. Caesar's *The Gallic War* was written around 50 B.C., but the earliest manuscript we have comes from A.D. 850, 900 years later—no one questions this document's authenticity. The *Histories* of Tacitus, written in A.D. 100, originally came in 41 books, of which only 14 survive. The Roman history of Livy (*Ab Urbe condita*) originally appeared in 142 books, of which only 35 manuscripts survive. More than 5,000 manuscripts of the New Testament have survived from the ancient world.[4]

3. *The story is self-authenticating. The manner in which it is related demonstrates the truthfulness of the accounts*—that is, the inconsistencies help to authenticate these books as actual records of what people experienced. We must remember that these are *eyewitness* accounts. Ask a trial lawyer about what people say in court when they give their eyewitness accounts and the lawyer will help you discover a fact about human nature: *The stories always vary*, because human perception is individual and personal. Listen to a group of people describe witnessing a car accident. As one tells about seeing the automobiles crash, the others start adding details about traffic lights, other vehicles, a dog in the middle of the street, and so on. As it turns out, the first witness telling the story only has a partial version of what occurred. Others add what they saw and the story grows. Because it is

untrue? No, because as it is authentic, additional
details surface. In the Gospels, we read about real-life
encounters told by people who saw things from their
unique perspectives. The details of these encounters
defy the grasp of any one observer. It takes four writers to tell us what happened! Their differences vali-
date the story.

We only have one book that tells us the whole story line,
that pulls together the various accounts to establish what
exactly happened: the Bible. From authenticated and reliable
pages, we can conclude that Jesus of Nazareth was definitely
crucified. The Gospel accounts also agree that Jesus was resurrected from the dead, and that He sent His followers out to tell
the amazing news across the entire world. This evidence is clear,
firm and credible. This is the story.

Now, what does the story mean? For an answer we must
press on for a theological perspective.

Notes
1. Two of the oldest and best Greek manuscripts containing the Gospel of Mark,
   Codex Vaticanus and Codex Sinaiticus, end at verse 16:8. Even many conservative
   biblical scholars, however, reject this shorter ending. As a compromise, verses
   9 through 20 are included in most modern translations, with a note indicating
   the discrepancy.
2. "7Q5" at Wikipedia.org. http://en.wikipedia.org/wiki/7Q5 (accessed September
   2007).
3. A. T. Robertson, *Luke the Historian in the Light of Research* (New York: C. Scribner
   Sons, 1920).
4. S. F. F. Bruce, *The New Testament Documents: Are They Reliable?* (Grand Rapids, MI:
   Eerdmans Publishing Co., 1970), p. 20.

What Does It Say About God?

Cruising leisurely through high school, Wayne Booshada was a typical kid who hadn't set foot in a church for four years. Seventeen-year-old Wayne's typical teenage interests tilted toward rock 'n' roll, and religious stuff just wasn't on the list. Musically talented with an excellent singing voice, Wayne also loved to play guitar.

One evening, a friend invited Wayne to a youth meeting in a Methodist church in Dallas, Texas; Wayne showed up because there wasn't much else to do. For the evening's program they played a recorded sermon by Peter Marshall, Chaplain of the United States Senate and an important minister in a large Presbyterian church in Washington D.C. Wayne settled in for another one of those pit-stop delays before racing on with his teenage life.

Much to Wayne's surprise, Peter Marshall talked about Jesus Christ as if He were a real person who Marshall knew, talked with and sought guidance from in making his life decisions. Intrigued, Wayne listened intently to the sermon. It sounded like Peter Marshall was describing a living person he'd just had coffee with, and this stirred Wayne's imagination. Could someone actually know a man who had lived nearly 2,000 years ago as if He were a friend from across the street? Wayne didn't know what to think.

The recording sent Wayne on a personal search. When he'd get home from school, before doing his homework, he'd read a chapter in the Bible. That didn't prove easy—the only Bible around was an old copy of the *King James Version*, which seemed rather obscure and dense, but Wayne persisted. At the end of the reading, he would say the Lord's Prayer, because it seemed like a ritual of some sort that might help in trying to figure out how Peter Marshall developed such an amazing relationship with this Jesus. Lurking in the back of Wayne's mind remained the burning question of whether or not God was actually real. Maybe the God talk was all fantasy. While he didn't understand these issues, he continued to seek answers.

After a month of going through the same ritual every day, one night Wayne went to bed and drifted off to dreamland. Somewhere in the night, he heard his name called. Awaking from a deep sleep, he sat up in bed and called out, "What?" When no one answered, Wayne assumed that he must have been dreaming and went back to sleep.

The next day Wayne went through his regular routine of homework, Bible study, and the Lord's Prayer. Once again, he went to bed as usual and quickly fell asleep. Again, Wayne heard his name called in a personal and forceful manner. Startled by the déjà vu of this second experience, he woke up and decided that his mother must be calling him. Wayne called out to her but didn't get an answer. He concluded that, again, he must have been dreaming and ignored the experience.

On the third night, Wayne followed the identical format and went to sleep, but he kept in mind what had occurred the previous nights. When he heard his name called again, he knew something important was happening. He concluded that God was calling him, just as the Lord had done to others throughout the Bible. No longer could he ignore that call.

Wayne answered aloud, "Lord, what do You want?" With even more confidence, he called out, "Here I am!"

At that moment, Wayne felt a presence move into and fill his room. While he still today finds the experience difficult to describe, he could literally feel his hair stand on end. Wayne knew that Jesus Christ had entered his room, and there was no question in his mind that He was moving toward the bed. Wayne realized that Jesus was not only looking straight at him but *through* him, and understood everything the young man had done during his entire life. Yet even though Jesus knew every wrong deed, there was no condemnation. Love remained and prevailed. In astonishment at what was happening, Wayne reached out to feel the robe Jesus wore. The experience was vivid and electric.

"I'm not happy with how I am running my life," Wayne blurted out. From somewhere deep within him the words bubbled up: "Would You come in and take over my life?"

At the moment he said those words, Wayne felt completely immersed inside and out with what today he can only call "liquid love." A heavenly benevolence, charity and peacefulness enveloped him. Songs exploded in his ears beyond any sound he had ever heard before. Love and happiness shot through Wayne in undulating waves of overwhelming joy. Never before had Wayne experienced anything like this moment! The exhilaration was so profound and total that he began to weep.

When Wayne Booshada woke up the next morning, he didn't have language to describe what had happened to him. Words like "regeneration," "new birth" and "born again" weren't yet a part of his vocabulary, but Wayne knew everything was different. He hadn't yet learned about the meaning of words like "resurrection" and "justification," but for the first time in his life, he had spiritual eyes. Wayne Booshada had encountered the resurrected Christ.

The Beginnings of Theology

While Wayne's story cannot be scientifically verified, he has faithfully lived more than four decades in accord with and in response to this experience. His fidelity to the remarkable event stands as its own validation.

As people in the Early Church had similar experiences, the Church Fathers attempted to deduce general principles about God and His relationship to people from such encounters. Today, we call their deductions and the statements they made about them "Christian theology."

To develop a complete context for the resurrection event, we must look at theological expressions from across the centuries and consider them. These faith statements tell us what learned and disciplined Christians have concluded during various periods of history.

If Wayne's story had occurred in A.D. 50, it might well have been one of the events noted by the Fathers. However, the Church has always given priority to what was recorded in the Bible. Because these first stories are those of the Apostles, who were eyewitnesses of Jesus' life and ministry, their accounts are considered normative and authoritative. When we explore Christian theology, we are reflecting on the meaning of various people's experiences in light of the Apostles' experiences recorded in Scripture.

To develop a complete context for the resurrection event, we must look at theological expressions from across the centuries and consider them. So what do 20 centuries of Christian thinkers believe the crucifixion and resurrection say about God and us?

So what do 20 centuries of Christian thinkers believe the crucifixion and resurrection say about God and us?

The Crucifixion of Jesus

Christian theologians have always contended that we can't understand the death of Jesus without embracing His resurrection—and neither can we grasp the resurrection without exploring the reasons for the crucifixion. There are some religious groups that affirm that Jesus died without believing that He rose again, but the historic Church maintains that these people can never understand the redemptive meaning of His death until they explore what followed on Easter morning. By the same token, some Christian denominations hurry past Jesus' agonizing death and reject the crucifix as a symbol of evil, while rushing forward to embrace the Easter sunrise. They miss the fullness of the glorious resurrection because they don't remember the figure hanging on the cross.

The earliest theologians concluded that we must start with Jesus' death on Good Friday if we are to understand the theological meaning of His resurrection on the third day. Here are a few biblical keys to be considered:

1. *Jesus anticipated His death.* Even before the resurrection of Lazarus, Jesus said, "For this reason the Father loves me, because I lay down my life, that I may take it up again. No one takes it from me, but I lay it down of my own accord; I have the power to lay it down, and I have the power to take it again;

this charge I have received from my Father" (John 10:17-18, *NASB*).

In this passage we see that Jesus anticipated His resurrection and tied His death and rising together. He had a choice about His death and was in control of the final situation. As the hour of His death approached, Jesus made it clear that He was moving forward of His own free will. He said to Peter in the Garden of Gethsemane, "Put your sword into its sheath; shall I not drink the cup which the Father has given me?" (John 18:11) Jesus expected crucifixion

2. *His death had a divine purpose.* Jesus' public ministry began with His baptism by John the Baptist. At that moment, John the Baptist proclaimed, "Behold the Lamb of God, who takes away the sin of the world!" (John 1:29, *NASB*). At the Last Supper, only hours before His death, Jesus took the elements of the annual Jewish Passover feast and gave them new meaning. The bread and wine were now symbols of His body and blood, to be given for the forgiveness of sin. Just as the unleavened bread and wine were offered around the table, His body would be extended to the world as the ultimate symbol of the coming kingdom of God.

3. *The intentional death of Jesus on the cross was on our behalf,* even in the midst of our indifference and unconcern. Just before Jesus was taken captive in the Garden of

Gethsemane, He prayed that this final act of His earthly ministry would have a consecrating effect on His disciples. He prayed, "Sanctify them in the truth; thy word is truth. As thou didst sent me into the world, so I have sent them into the world. And for their sake I consecrate myself, that they also may be consecrated in truth" (John 17:17-19).

The profound impact of the crucifixion of Jesus *did* change His Apostles, but it was not until well after His death that they began to realize the result. How could this be? Because Jesus substituted His obedience for their and our disobedience, His wholeness for human brokenness. It is significant that Wayne Booshada knew his own unworthiness the very moment he experienced the holiness of Jesus Christ entering his bedroom—he immediately asked Jesus to make his life whole. When we truly encounter Jesus' divine love, we realize our lack. The apostle Paul recognized this fact when he wrote, "For as by one man's disobedience many were made sinners, so by one man's obedience many will be made righteous" (Rom. 5:19).

4. *The cross consummated Jesus' earthly ministry.* Never before in human history had anyone offered himself as a sacrifice for all human sinfulness. While Jesus taught highly ethical and moral standards, His role as teacher was not ultimate—just as His healing ministry, in the end, was more than restoring sick and broken people. These amazing teachings and deeds

were the prelude to the main event. He issued an opening blow to death when He raised up Lazarus, Jairus's daughter and others, but the Evil One had used death as his scourge on the human race for too long, and Jesus' ultimate intention was to defeat the Defeater. This goal demanded His death.

Paul stated the sweeping meaning of Jesus' ministry in these terms: "For the love of Christ controls us, because we are convinced that one has died for all; therefore all have died. And he died for all that those who live might live no longer for themselves but for him who for their sake died and was raised" (2 Cor. 5:14-15).

5. *Jesus' death gave us the capacity to become more than we ever thought possible,* in spite of our mistakes and arrogant behavior. The transforming effect of the death of Jesus Christ has, for 2,000 years, turned self-preoccupied people away from their bent toward selfishness, and caused a metamorphosis that has given us the ability to love unselfishly. The mystery of His redemptive suffering altered the course of human history. He, indeed, did give Himself as a ransom for many (see Mark 10:45).

The Resurrection of Jesus

Once we are clear that Jesus was not just a passionate teacher trying to reform society or a broken religious system, and that He ended up making some folks angry and getting killed, we are in a position to understand that His restoration to life was the vindication of all that He said and did. Not only did Jesus fall down to the mat from what seemed like a final knockout blow, willing to stake His life on the Good News He had come to bring—but also, after the fight, He returned fully and gloriously restored.

What happened in the dark of night and death?

There is no answer. A response is impossible. No one saw the actual moment of resurrection. The event remains a truly transcendent, otherworldly event. In a real and fundamental sense, the resurrection surpassed human experience and entered into another order of existence. It is a mystery.

A mystery is an event or situation that defies all human analogies, which means that we have no language to capture what happened. We don't have words that can explain the facts. As Jesus stepped out of the tomb on that first Easter morning, it was the last phase in a process that even to this day we do not understand. We are forced to turn from trying to explain how it happened to talking about what it means.

The resurrection fulfilled the promises of the past, all the messianic prophecies of the Hebrew Scriptures. Throughout the history of the Jewish race, the hope for a messiah had persisted in every heart. Regardless of various political circumstances spanning several thousand years, Jews looked for one who would vindicate their hopes. The New Testament tells us that Jesus used very specific language to indicate that He was the One for whom they had waited, and at the same time, redefined what the Messiah had come to accomplish. Later, when Paul proclaimed the message of Jesus to the Gentile world, he

The death of Jesus set the world free from the shackles of sin that bound the human race to failure and destruction. His resurrection opened the door to a new future. Anyone who started down the path from the empty tomb could walk into a new tomorrow, infused with the changing power of Jesus' life.

carefully noted that Jesus fulfilled everything promised to the Jews in the past. When Jesus stepped out of the tomb on Easter morning, the dreams of the prophets and sages of Israel came true. What Moses, David, Elijah, Jeremiah and a host of other godly visionaries had prayed for was now finished.

The resurrection fulfilled aspirations for the future. As we have observed, the death of Jesus set the world free from the shackles of sin that bound the human race to failure and destruction. As that freedom was accomplished by His death, His resurrection opened the door to a new future. Anyone who started down the path from the empty tomb could walk into a new tomorrow, infused with the changing power of Jesus' life. Just as Jesus came out of death with a new body, we too can be new. Paul explained the promise to the Gentile world by saying, "For if we have been united with him in a death like his [for us, baptism], we shall certainly be united with him in a resurrection like his" (Rom. 6:5).

The resurrection prepared the way for our resurrection. What lies ahead for the followers of Jesus Christ is not a general expectation but a specific promise. Just as Christ was raised, so too shall believers be raised. Paul wrote, "But now is Christ risen from the dead, and become the firstfruits of them that slept. For since by man came death, by man came also the resurrection of the dead . . . in Christ shall all be made alive" (1 Cor. 15:20-22, *KJV*). The promise here is that we will experience the same resurrection at the end of the age.

Jewish theology experienced an unfolding and gradually expanding understanding of what happened in death. During Old Testament times, their expectation for existence after death was *Sheol* (*Hades* in Greek), something like living in a dim, murky cave. Though better than non-existence, *Sheol* still wasn't too promising.

The first Christian believers recognized that during the three days in the tomb, Jesus Christ descended to *Sheol*. When the Apostles Creed (the earliest full affirmation of faith) was compiled in the second century, it proclaimed, "he descended into hell." The apostle Peter indicates that Jesus preached the Good News of redemption to those who had departed from the beginnings of time (see 1 Pet. 3:18-20).

The Apostles and other early believers were announcing that everything about eternity was changed after Jesus Christ's descent into *Sheol*. No longer would the shape of our future be positive only in some general, undefined sense. Rather, believers could look toward their own resurrections into glorious, transformed bodies Jesus prepared the way and was the proto type of what is to come for each of us.

The Good News

Whether the account comes from the apostle Paul or a con temporary disciple such as Wayne Booshada, the report of a personal encounter with Jesus Christ can be received as goods news about God's relationship with humankind. The earliest Christian message was a straightforward, simple statement relating the death and resurrection of Jesus Christ. While fully grasping how exactly it had happened was wrapped in mystery, the facts were so basic that a child could understand them—but it would take the rest of one's life to internalize the theological promises bound up in those facts. And that was the point:

Believing the story only began the journey, and that journey would open them to receive the fullness of complete love and eternal hope.

Still recognizing that life is filled with unavoidable illness, unexpected misfortune and undeserved tragedy, the first followers of Jesus Christ knew that beyond the momentary defeat of the cross was eternal victory. Rather than living for revenge, they became people of forgiveness. No longer harboring resentment, they acquired freedom from ill will and indignation. Liberated from a fear of death, believers waved goodbye as their loved ones died, looking forward to reunion beyond the veil of death.

Seeing the Risen Christ

The appearances recorded in Matthew, Mark, Luke and John weren't all there was to the story of the resurrection. Many times during the past 2,000 years, beyond the book of Acts, people have described their own encounters with the resurrected Lord. He has never ceased to appear! How do we make sense out of such claims?

Let's go back to the Greek texts and sort out what happened.

Whether the passages are translated "Jesus appeared" or "Jesus revealed Himself," the Greek word used in John's Gospel to describe what the observers saw after the resurrection is *phaneroo*, a non-theological term for an experience that is visible to sensory perception. In other words, witnesses saw Jesus with their eyes. In the Gospels, as well as Paul's dissertation on the resurrection in 1 Corinthians 15, *phaneroo* expresses events seen with the eyes.

The appearances didn't happen in a vision, a psychological projection or in their faith, hopes and dreams. These people observed the event in the same way they saw the sun coming up in the morning. The sun rising and the Son rising were observed in the same fashion.

Phaneroo also implies that perception of what was seen was understood. In other words, what was looked at with the eyes must also have been understood with the mind. The bottom line is that the people described in the New Testament observed Jesus like they would have seen anything else in their world, and understood what they were seeing.

And yet . . . there are differences.

On the Road to Damascus

While on his way to Damascus to attack followers of "The Way," a light flashed from heaven and Saul was confronted by a heavenly vision. When Saul asked who spoke to him, he received a highly significant answer: "I am Jesus, whom you are persecuting" (Acts 9:1-6).

Saul met Jesus on the dusty road to his own destiny.

Notice what followed. The men with Saul heard the voice, but didn't see Jesus. Something happened to Saul that was beyond the experience of his companions. Obviously, Jesus Christ has His own unique ways of making Himself known to His people—even when they are surrounded by others who notice nothing at all.

Jesus in Hollywood

Karen Zablocki was 26 years old when *Jesus Christ Superstar* grabbed national headlines. Across America, people were talking about Andrew Lloyd Webber's rock opera that portrayed the ministry and crucifixion of Jesus. Karen and her husband, Walter, lived in Long Beach, California, when the showing of *Superstar* was featured at the Hollywood Bowl. There was no way they were going to let that chance pass them by!

Karen had grown up in church and on a number of occasions had been emotionally moved during worship services, but there had always been some distance between her and the Christian message. She certainly wasn't a doubter—she believed in Jesus and the Bible and was more in the category of an indifferent church member. Still, the idea of seeing Webber's sell-out production had a particular fascination for her. Advertising was everywhere. Television constantly promoted ticket sales, but it was something more that held her attention. Karen couldn't put her finger on it, but she increasingly felt that she and Walter must go. For reasons she couldn't identify, Karen hungered to see what *Jesus Christ Superstar* would tell her.

Under an expansive blue sky, the audience sat in the gentle breeze to enjoy the production. On this particular evening, the actors were dressed in costumes of the period and sang with professional expertise. The lights and colors were dazzling.

The show proved to be more than Karen had hoped. As scene followed scene, the musical came to the moment when reporters hound Jesus for a headline story. The audience watched the approach of twentieth-century mass media imposed on a first-century story. The song in this scene expresses the pushiness of the press as journalists harass Jesus for a news story.

Karen's blood started to boil as the reporters bore down on Jesus with no sense of reverence or respect for Him. For reasons she couldn't explain, Karen felt offended that Jesus was treated like a football, kicked around by mad-dog journalists. She sensed that everything about this scene was wrong, and it made her want to defend Jesus. She felt like her best friend was under

The resurrection suggests that we live in two worlds, one physical and the other spiritual. The facts of the resurrection tell us that the risen Christ brought these worlds together when He set foot outside the tomb. He has one foot in both worlds, and He continues to bring the things of God into our time and space.

attack. Karen wanted to run down and protect Him. She was mortified at the treatment He was receiving.

At that moment, it happened. Before Karen's eyes, the actor playing the role of Jesus began to change. His face took on new features and his eyes became a different shape. Karen gasped. She was not seeing an actor, but Jesus Christ. The real, authentic Jesus! Karen knew this was the "flesh and blood" Jesus, resurrected from the dead and looking up into the audience at her. As surely as her husband was sitting next to her, Jesus Christ was looking up at her with the same compassionate eyes the Scriptures revealed.

Karen's mouth dropped open and she froze in her seat. Slowly, Jesus Christ disappeared and faded away, and the actor reappeared and continued his role. Karen sat transfixed, unable to move. She didn't know what had occurred, but she had no question that she had encountered the Lord who had reached across the centuries to step into her life. She had seen Jesus Christ.

For a while Karen didn't tell anyone, but she knew that the encounter had ignited a change in her life from the inside out. A new relationship with Jesus took root and she had to nourish it. One of the pressing needs Karen felt was an urgency to know Jesus even better and more deeply. A couple of her friends told Karen about something called Bible Study Fellowship, and she enrolled in the course. From that moment forward, Karen became an ardent student of the Bible. Knowing Jesus Christ through His Word is an imperative in her life to this day. A resurrection discovery changed everything about how Karen saw the world.

Just like Karen's, Saul's experience of seeing Christ was not matched by anyone around him. He saw a *phaneroo* that was not shared by anyone else. His experience was particular to the moment, but it left him with the certainty that he had encountered Christ. Paul based the rest of his life on that certainty.

The Two Worlds

The resurrection suggests that we live in two worlds, one physical and the other spiritual. Both surround us all the time, but we see only one of them. But the facts of the resurrection also tell us that the risen Christ brought these worlds together when He set foot outside the tomb. After being raised, Jesus was physically able to go back and forth between these two realms, between here and eternity, at will. His sudden appearances—*phaneroo*—are a firm indication that He has one foot in both worlds, and that He continues to bring the things of God into our time and space.

Are we ready to live in both worlds? Are we ready to see Him?

PART THREE

The Results
A.D. 85

Blessed be the God and Father of our Lord Jesus Christ!
By his great mercy we have been born anew to a
living hope through the resurrection of Jesus Christ from
the dead. . . . In this you rejoice, though now for
a little while you may have to suffer various trials.

1 PETER 1:3-6

The evening sun drifted slowly beneath the horizon. Even though the darkness of night was coming quickly, the heat of summer lingered across the Cappadocian plains. The old man sat at the table eating as his two friends watched through an open window outside the flat-roofed house.

"He eats slowly," Achim said.

"John is getting old," Boaz responded. "He has had a hard day. Many people were here to listen to his teaching."

Achim nodded his head. "Yes, the crowd grows each day."

"Dare we speak to him?"

Achim shrugged. "Why not? John never resents questions. After all, we have been at his right hand all this time and helped with every need."

Boaz slowly walked to the door and slipped inside. Old John's black hair had turned gray and his arms had become thin. His body still had a wiry, muscular quality, but the apostle no longer looked as vigorous as he sounded when he taught. Boaz was reluctant to approach him, but he was already inside the room.

"Ah, Boaz!" John looked up. "Come in." The old man patted the tabletop. "Sit down."

Achim slipped in and dropped down on the bench across from John. Boaz sat down beside him with more reserve.

"Sir," Boaz began, "I wondered . . . you don't seem to resent the pressure of the crowd that stays here hour after hour. At your age . . . I mean . . . it must be demanding work. Why do you push yourself so hard?"

John smiled. "It was after the resurrection, you see. Up by the Sea of Tiberias that Jesus appeared to us. Simon Peter, Thomas, Nathanael, the sons of Zebedee and several others. He came out to the edge of the lake and spoke directly to me."

John stopped and looked down in the bowl. The memory had touched a nerve. "He said that when I was young, I dressed myself . . . but when I was old I would stretch out my hands and someone else would gird me." John's face turned haunted and uncertain. "I never understood . . ." the old man's face brightened abruptly, ". . . but I did know what the Lord meant when He told me to feed His sheep." He smiled at the two across the table. "That's what I do every day. Feed His sheep."

"You do this work with such determination," Achim said. "How can you stay at the task with such fidelity?"

"How?" John laughed. "It is not hard. The resurrection changed everything."

Reality

The resurrection did not occur to end up as a statement in a creed or a lesson in a children's Sunday School class. The event was not meant to become a belief as much as it was a redefinition of human existence. Not that's it unimportant as a conviction . . . but the resurrection of Jesus Christ had a far more sweeping impact. We were intended to enter into its mystery in order to acquire the gifts that the resurrection offers us.

We do not define the resurrection as much as it defines us. And as it does, our lives are transformed. We experience the results of the resurrection.

Throughout the Gospels, as well as in Paul's dissertation on the resurrection in 1 Corinthians 15, *phaneroo* (discussed in chapter 6) is used to indicate an event seen with the eyes, experienced in a real and tangible way. When passages containing this Greek word are translated with the English words "manifested" or "revealed," we are intended to understand that what was hidden or not previously seen had now come to light. For those whose experiences were recorded in the Gospels, a real Person was standing before them, demanding genuine response.

Chapter 7

The apostle Paul had a different sort of encounter on the Damascus road. The risen Jesus manifested Himself in a brilliant light that flashed from heaven. Paul was knocked to the ground and a voice said, "I am Jesus, whom you are persecuting" (Acts 9:5, *NIV*).

Paul's experience was something new: While an understanding of the resurrection dawned on him similar to that experienced by those who saw Jesus before His ascension, Christ revealed—manifested—Himself differently. After his encounter with the risen Lord, Saul (soon to be Paul) was taken to the house of Judas, where Ananias came to explain what had happened. After Ananias prayed for his sight to return, Paul was baptized and continued on his way a changed man. The rest of his life was spent explaining the meaning of the resurrection.

Paul believed to his core that his identity, meaning, personal direction and destiny—in other words, his entire reality—were completely changed when he encountered the risen Christ, and that the same possibility is available to all who seek the living Lord. Christ has made a way for each person to follow Him out of the empty tomb into a new reality of life.

We must realize that it is still possible for Jesus to reveal Himself in new and unexpected ways. Is it possible to see Jesus as the apostle John did, by the Sea of Tiberias? I believe the answer is yes. Is it conceivable that you could meet Him as Paul did? Yes! Is it possible that Jesus might come to you in other ways? In dreams? In a vision? In a spiritual experience? Absolutely! Jesus the Christ, risen bodily from the dead, desires to reveal Himself to each one of us and change our reality.

We must realize that it is still

possible for Jesus to reveal Himself

in new and unexpected ways.

Jesus the Christ, risen bodily from

the dead, desires to reveal

Himself to each one of us

and change our reality.

Personal Reality Shift

Remember the story of Wayne Booshada in chapter 5? We explored the turning point in Wayne's life, when he answered the call of God he heard in the night. Jesus Christ came into his bedroom and Wayne's life was forever different. But that's not the whole story.

A year and a half after his late-night encounter with Jesus, Wayne Booshada went to an evening church service at Cockerill Hill Methodist Church in Dallas, Texas. By that time, he had been baptized and been discipled through some of Billy Graham's resources. He had also picked up a copy of the spiritual biography of Thomas Merton, and that had significantly impacted his life. In addition, a young man named Bob Stamps, his church's youth pastor, had added a great deal to Wayne's life. He was continuing to grow and sensed a desire for a more powerful encounter with Jesus Christ.

On this particular evening in Dallas, Pastor Jack Gray had preached a moving sermon and the congregation was spiritually charged. As he came to the conclusion of the service, Pastor Gray said, "I believe there are two people here that the Lord wants to touch. I'm not going to pray . . . the Lord is just going to be with you. You know who you are and I'm inviting you to come to the altar of the church."

In that moment, Wayne Booshada knew that he was one of the people Jack Gray was talking about. Without further prompting, Wayne jumped to his feet and raced to the kneeling rail in front of the altar. Dropping to his knees, he began praying fervently. Pouring out his heart, he asked the Lord

Jesus to fill him with His presence.

In the months prior, Wayne had heard people talking about the gifts of the Spirit, but he wasn't seeking some unusual gift. He prayed, "Lord, I don't care if I ever speak in tongues or have any other special gift; I just want more of You."

As he prayed, Wayne realized that Jesus was standing on the other side of the altar rail. The risen Christ was right there in front of him! The experience was so real and personal that Wayne gasped, breathless as Jesus reached out to put His hands on the young man's head. Abruptly, a wave of love shot through Wayne's body. After a few seconds, a wave of peace worked through his being. This was followed by an extraordinary outpouring of power. Again and again, the tangible, undulating waves of love, peace and power surged through Wayne. For 10 to 15 minutes, the outpouring came with such force that he couldn't stand up or walk. All Wayne could do was lie on the floor as this new inner reality worked its way into him. For 30 minutes, he was delirious with a sense of love, compelling love, working in him. The hands of Jesus Christ had sent an extraordinary new dimension of reality into the very core of his life.

Wayne's sense of purpose would be forever different because of this encounter with the risen Christ. During the era of the Jesus Movement, Wayne Booshada traveled across America playing his guitar, singing spiritual songs and sharing the message of Jesus Christ. Later, he planted churches that still exist across the United States. In time, Wayne became a bishop in the Communion of Evangelical Episcopal Churches, and today he is an archbishop who oversees the work of bishops and priests who touch the lives of thousands of people.

It made a big difference! Bishop Wayne Booshada's reality shifted and his life was transformed as he came to a new and profound understanding of the resurrection.

Global Change from a Personal Reality Shift

Periodically, entire societies experience a shift in their reality, and sometimes these changes in values and ideas can be traced to a single person. For example, consider what happened in the twelfth century.

The Roman Empire had faded by the fifth century and the currency-based economy of organized civilization had failed. The standard of exchange disappeared in the collapse of the dissolving world order. No longer did Roman *denarii* serve as the primary medium of commerce. Disorder filled the marketplace and the only way to transact business became bartering.

Business was done on an exchange basis of one item for another. For example, let's say that you brought a chicken to market, while I brought a hunk of beef. If you wanted beef and I wanted chicken, we might argue back and forth until I persuaded you to throw in a dozen eggs to make the deal square. Trading meant bargaining until an acceptable level of exchange was achieved.

Obviously, it was difficult for anyone to accumulate much, but life during the medieval period was simple, as long as you kept your expectations low. Time moved with very few interruptions. Day in and day out, people rocked along with little more excitement than the sun coming up every morning and going down every night.

By the year 1200, however, things were changing. A new money economy was emerging, and a new merchant class along with it. Once again, merchants could become rich by compiling wealth. In fact, a merchant in central Italy named Pietro de Bernadone stood on the threshold of a fortune. All he needed was the cooperation of his son to perpetuate the business, and the Bernadones could dominate the cloth business. There was only one problem: Pietro's son, Giovanni, didn't seem to understand the meaning of opportunity.

Smitten with medieval notions about the romance of war, the boy went off to fight. He expected the fun and frivolity that he constantly pursued, but instead he spent a year as a prisoner of war in Perugia. When he was finally released, he was in bad shape—he came home wounded. As he recovered, he became much more serious and spiritually oriented, and was drawn to show compassion and mercy to those with leprosy. But something even more profound was churning in his head. The times were changing, and Giovanni was increasingly uncomfortable with his father's values. Was his life to be governed by the pursuit of money or was there something more valuable to pursue? What was the right path to take?

While visiting the tiny old church of St. Damian, Giovanni had a remarkable experience. In the center of the church hung a large crucifix with the figure of Christ in the center. Giovanni heard a voice speaking from the crucifix and it gave him a very specific command.

"Rebuild My Church," Christ directed.

Giovanni's reality shifted. He had discovered a burning reality that motivated his entire existence. He began to gather stones to literally rebuild the building's worn structure, even returning to his father's warehouse to sell valuable cloth to raise money for his project.

When his father, Pietro, discovered what he considered the folly of selling Bernadone cloth to pay for the renovation of the dilapidated building, he dragged the boy before the bishop to renounce him. To the shock of all, Giovanni stripped off all his clothing and marched out of the church naked, renouncing the materialism of his father. Giovanni, also called Francesco, had discovered a higher reality.

Today we call him St. Francis of Assisi.

Stories about St. Francis abound. Perhaps one of the most astonishing is about the time he encountered a leper begging by the roadside. Overcome with compassion for the poor man, Francis Bernadone stopped his horse, jumped off, kissed the disfigured man and then remounted to continue his journey. When he looked back, the leper had become Jesus Christ.

In every possible way, St. Francis set out to become an imitator of Christ. Wherever he went, people were profoundly touched by his compassion, joy and wisdom. While he was not a great organizer or administrator, the impact of his life laid the foundation for one of the most important monastic movements in history. The Franciscans were eventually to leave an indelible mark on the entire history of Western civilization. After Columbus discovered the New World, the first missionaries to the new hemisphere were the Franciscans, the monastic order founded by St. Francis. Christianity first entered the Americas because a cloth merchant's son found a higher reality than his father, or anyone else, ever imagined. His encounter with the

When we encounter the risen One,

we learn that our heavenly Father

created us with a purpose—that we

are His image-bearers, created to

be shaped into Christ's likeness.

The resurrection reaches into the void

that lurks in each of our lives and fills it.

Our identity is established.

risen Christ shifted Francis's reality in a way that continues to touch and transform countless numbers of people today.

The Elements of a Reality Shift

Every person who profoundly encounters the risen Lord will undergo a recalibration of his or her identity, meaning, personal direction and destiny. Each of these dimensions is an important focus for us to grasp. The resurrection can redefine us in the same ways.

Identity

Paul's Damascus road experience was so powerful that his name was changed from Saul to Paul. He was transformed from a protector of the old Jewish way into a proclaimer of the new way of Christ. To his death, Paul remained a Jew and a supporter of the Jewish people, but an important new dimension was added to who he was. His identity was reformed around the risen Christ.

As the New Testament story unfolds, we catch glimpses of this same phenomenon again and again. The lives of new believers were irreversibly impacted by the resurrection. Their identities were changed; they became different people. After the New Testament period, this metamorphosis on the heels of an encounter with Jesus continued. Many Christians chose death at the hands of the Roman Empire over renouncing their new identities, but as more and more citizens defined themselves by their faith rather than national loyalty, the entire Roman world was changed.

In reflecting on the human story, I sometimes think that we are originally created without a definite sense of identity, that we must work out who we are through the process of living. At birth, we seem to be a lump of clay awaiting final molding. During and immediately after adolescence, the quest for identity is paramount. As the shape settles into place, we gain a firmer sense of identity, allowing our lives to move forward.

Later in life, after a divorce or the death of a loved one or similar catastrophic event, we are often pushed into a redefinition of who we are. It's difficult to understand how important identity is until yours is shaken. As a child, I was adopted into a family in which I didn't fit well. Through my teenage years, I struggled to understand my own uniqueness, but it wasn't until mid-life that I recovered a clear sense of who I really was. I had a gnawing, undefined void that occasionally left me with significant uncertainty. Remembering that time, I know how vital it is to have a well-defined sense of who you are. Identity is crucial.

The resurrection of Jesus Christ has deep implications for how we understand who we are. When we encounter the risen One, we learn that our heavenly Father created us with a purpose—that we are His image-bearers, created to be shaped into Christ's likeness. The resurrection reaches into the void that lurks in each of our lives and fills it. Our identity is established.

Meaning

The Gospel stories suggest that the Apostles saw themselves as little more than average Jews trying to scratch out an existence in a tough world occupied by a tyrannical empire. The highest level of their hopes was to see the Messiah come to lead them out of Rome's bondage. When they met Jesus, they missed the meaning of most of what He taught—they didn't understand that life in God meant much more than eking out a living and escaping the oppressor.

When we read these stories, we tend to miss the meaning, too. Most of us see ourselves in much the same light as the Apostles saw themselves. We don't see ourselves as eternally significant people, created to do the work and will of God on earth. Instead, we hope to float along through life with the maximum of creaturely comforts and a minimum of tragedy. Bad things happen to good people, so we know we'll get some rough times—but we hope to slide under the door without it hitting us too hard. We're hopeful people, sure . . . but not highly significant.

Does that seem about right?

The resurrection story slams into us, as it did the Apostles, and tells us that life is much more than simply surviving: We are called to be part of God's kingdom breaking into history. In the eyes of God, we're big-time players! Jesus Christ sees us as unique, valuable and irreplaceable. He stepped out of the grave on our behalf!

Over the years in my counseling work with hurting teenagers, I've found that the vast majority do not feel any sense of personal value. For a thousand reasons, they see themselves as without significance and of no account. When kids struggle with low self-esteem, the natural outcome is destructive behavior. Often they flounder into drug use, seeking an escape from their emptiness. Because they see no ultimate meaning to their lives, they see no reason to value themselves.

Value is something we must claim for ourselves, and it is tied to an understanding about the meaningfulness of our lives. When our reality shifts as we stand by the tomb and hear Jesus say, "I have arisen for *you!*" it suddenly makes perfect sense to treat ourselves as valuable. As the Son comes up, the sun rises on a new person, full of meaning and purpose.

Meaning is *that* important. We all must have it, and Christ's resurrection offers ultimate significance to each of our lives. It isn't important that we accomplish something big, but it *is* vital that we follow the path that He has laid down for us. Obedience to His direction imparts ultimate worth.

Personal Direction

The world is filled with people just like Wayne Booshada was as a teenager. They know there is a God and feel that they've made a beginning contact. They attend worship services with some frequency, but sense that something important is missing. They would like to have a greater sense of purpose, but aren't sure where to find it. What can they do?

Wayne's experience at the altar of Cockerill Hill Methodist Church offers a clue. Surrounded by voices proclaiming the possibility of special encounters with the Holy Spirit, Wayne came forward on that Sunday night seeking only a deeper relationship with Jesus. When the risen Christ appeared before him, Wayne received gifts of the Spirit, but more important, he engaged the Person of the risen Lord. Later, personal direction flowed from that discovery.

Not that personal direction isn't by itself a significant quest, but often it seems to be a by-product of meeting Jesus

Christ. He finds us and then we ask, "What is it You want?" His answer to that question gives us the direction we need.

On the other hand, many people live pointless lives without a sense of heading anywhere. They get up every morning and go to work, but beyond putting in their time, there is little point to what they do. A meeting with the risen Christ can radically change that approach to life and cause people to move ahead with a firm confidence that they are following the leading of God.

By and large, the Apostles were fishermen and laborers, people just trying to get by under the watchful eyes of the Romans. The height of their expectations was a good catch, a net full of fish. Their hopes didn't rise much beyond that horizon—yet today, their lives and deaths are commemorated in churches around the world. They wouldn't have believed you if you told them that the Roman Empire would eventually kneel before the Messiah they preached . . . but because they followed God's direction, it did!

If you need personal direction, look first for the risen Christ.

Destiny

Often the term "destiny" is applied to famous people like Napoleon, Lincoln or Roosevelt. We think of it as a word for people whose deeds are remembered in history books. While that is true, the human race has been shaped, molded and remolded by people we know little or nothing about. They, too, are equally people of destiny.

Our problem is that we hear affirmations and accolades without grasping their meaning. Psalm 100 says, "Know that the Lord is God! It is he that made us, and we are his; we are

Meeting the risen Christ always
changes how we see our lives.
The lights come on and we live with
a greater sense of destiny than we
ever dreamed possible. When we
discover that the risen Christ
desires a relationship with us,
we must conclude that we too
are persons of high calling.

his people, the sheep of his pasture . . . his steadfast love endures forever; his faithfulness to all generations" (vv. 3,5, *NIV*).

Do you find destiny in those words? Most people don't.

The psalmist claims that you didn't just *happen*, that you didn't just climb out of a protoplasmic ooze or drop out of the sky. You were designed, shaped and called into existence by the intention of God, who had you in mind from the beginning of creation. His steadfast love and faithfulness awaited your appearance before it could be fully poured out.

I'm talking about *you*.

Meeting the risen Christ always changes how we see our lives. The lights come on and we live with a greater sense of destiny than we ever dreamed possible. When we discover that the risen Christ desires a relationship with us, we must conclude that we too are persons of high calling.

The Ultimate Reality

Once encountered, the resurrection can provide the context for every other experience during our lifetime. The resurrection of Jesus Christ not only offers victory, but it also reaches into the depths of our most painful and tragic circumstances and surrounds them with unexpected hope and renewed promise.

The first letter of Peter points out that we "may have to suffer various trials" (1 Pet. 1:6). Some people seem to live with overpowering struggles for most of their lives. In the midst of that pain, the risen Christ declares, "Peace be with you. As the Father has sent me, even so I send you" (John 20:21).

Far from being people of illusion, believers hear Christ's call from the empty tomb to join Him on a very real journey toward wholeness, sanity and purpose. Whether the path we must walk is filled with rocks or is soft as sand, we can go forward knowing that we walk in the way of reality.

Can there be a greater road to travel?

CHAPTER 8

Insight

Insight. The power to see the truth of a situation. Discernment. Understanding.

When we have insight, we come to know something that previously eluded us, and now understand the subject with new comprehension. We no longer stand on the outside looking in, but go to the center of the subject with perception.

Some years ago, I wrote a book on deciphering dreams that was a product of years of attempting to get inside the world that opens up in our heads shortly after our heads hit the pillow. The Bible is filled with stories about God speaking through dreams, from Jacob's dream of a ladder into heaven to Joseph's dream-warning to take baby Jesus into Egypt. Yet my own dreams seemed impenetrable and impossible to understand at first. Many appeared silly, like crazy stories jumbled together without connection. Even though I knew dreams were important, I couldn't make any sense out of mine.

I kept approaching my dreams like an algebra problem. I thought that once I figured out what *a* was, I could add it to *b*, which would then equal *c*: a + b = c. Bingo!

Wrong.

Finally I began to realize that answers about dreams had to be discovered from a different direction. What I needed was intuitive reasoning, not deductive logic. I couldn't unravel dreams as if they were a math problem; I had to allow my inner personal experience—the place where dreams originate—to guide my understanding. In this way, insight developed.

For example, I had a situation at church that profoundly disturbed me. The problems circulated around a young man name George Carlton, whom I didn't trust. Day after day I sat at my office desk, fretting about this man and the problems he was causing. I clenched my fists and pounded on my desk. Then one night, I had a dream in which an old friend, Gene Warr, came roaring into the church parking lot, driving an army tank. He swung the tank around as if to blow the church building down. (Gene had in fact driven a tank during World War II.) In the dream, Gene said to me, "You are going to war!" (Or perhaps he said, "You are going to *Warr*," in classic dream word-replacement.)

As I studied the dream the next day, I suddenly and intuitively recognized that a deep part of me was confronting myself with the fact that I was on the edge of going to war with George Carlton, in a manner that could blow the church apart. Or to put it another way, the dream offered perception and insight into the depth of my anger, and warned me to tread cautiously.

Understanding this simple dream radically changed my approach to a real-life situation and brought an immediate adjustment in my behavior. I most certainly didn't want to get into a confrontation that would tear the church apart! Once the dream had given me understanding, I could more appropriately address the problem.

Insight.

Discernment in Darkness

Our lives are filled with a need for discernment. When we gain insight, we are able to make adjustments that allow us to live more effectively. The resurrection of Jesus Christ has produced this result in countless lives.

As people shifted from holding the resurrection as an idea or a doctrine to understanding it as a discovery of what was ultimate and final, their discernment shifted and changed. Insight into the meaning of the resurrection has the power and capacity to reorder direction, meaning and purpose. Let me tell you about how it affected Don Johnson.

Don spent his entire career as a United Methodist minister in the state of Oklahoma, and for a period of time was a district superintendent for that denomination. Originally from Texas, Don had always been a thoughtful, probing individual with a great sense of humor. At the same time, the shadow of tragic and devastating disasters troubled him. When he visited the USS *Arizona* in Pearl Harbor years after the terrible attack that compelled U.S. involved in World War II, Don was startled to find that the memorial to the deaths of American sailors left him shaken. *Why do assaults of this order occur?* he couldn't help but wonder. A sensitive man, it was part of his nature to be troubled by this unprovoked assault.

In the mid-'70s, Don and I took college-aged kids on a summer tour of Europe. One of our stops was at the Nazi concentration camp at Dachau, Germany. We walked through one of history's most disturbing places, where the extermination of human beings had been justified by political madness.

Our lives are filled with a need for discernment. When we gain insight, we are able to make adjustments that allow us to live more effectively. The resurrection of Jesus Christ has produced this result in countless lives. Insight into the meaning of the resurrection has the power and capacity to reorder direction, meaning and purpose.

The ovens used for cremation still stood at the back of the camp. No one in our group was left unaffected by this pit of despair.

Later, Don told me that what was running through his mind during the visit was the memory of a seminary experience. Klaus Tenzel, one of his seminary professors, had been a member of the Nazi Youth Corp. After the war, Tenzel had come to the United States to teach at Perkins School of Theology.

Standing before Don's class, Professor Tenzel had explained how, as a 12-year-old boy, he had been swept up in the German youth movement. In broken English, Tenzel confronted the class with these words: "Don't you understand dat zee God you prayed to for winning the war wast zee same God we prayed to every day in Germany? On different sides of the conflict, we both prayed to zee same God for victory. What shall we say about dis today?"

As we walked through the camp, Don couldn't stop thinking, *How could this be? The same God?* But suddenly, walking through the echoes of horror and unanswerable questions, Don became aware of Jesus standing beside him, in that place of utter darkness. The love and compassion of Christ swept over him, even as Don realized that the risen Lord was saying, "Take notice! Don't ever let this happen again!"

When Don walked out of the barbed-wire gates that day, he could only say, "I have seen the Lord. Right here in this hideous camp. I have seen Him clearly." Overpowered by the experience, Don couldn't express more, but he had gained discernment and knew he must do everything he could to prevent another such holocaust. The presence of the risen Christ had penetrated the layers of confusion and paralyzed inaction surrounding Don and given him insight for a way forward.

Clarity in Chaos

There's nothing new about misunderstanding in the midst of chaos. Perplexity has been with us as long as snow has fallen on the highest peaks. Yet a personal experience of Christ's resurrection has helped countless people find their way through situations that make no sense. In the last chapter, we saw that St. Francis of Assisi's insightful encounter with Christ opened a new path that guided multitudes to their own encounters. Here's another example of discovery emerging from a tunnel that seemed impossibly dark.

John Michael Talbot first burst on the American music scene as a 15-year-old country rock star with his brother, Terry, in a band called Mason Proffit. Performing with artists like The Grateful Dead, Jefferson Airplane and Janis Joplin sent his star to the top, and before long, he found himself in a world filled with drugs, booze and casual sex.

Even as he enjoyed his rapid rise to stardom, John began to hunger for spiritual reality. As he sought his own personal answers, a religious revival called the Jesus Movement began to surge across America. Hippies, druggies and dropouts were turning their lives in a new direction, and a powerful change moved across college campuses. It was a time of fresh discovery, and John somehow knew he needed discernment.

In 1971, he was on the road touring with Mason Proffitt when he checked into a Holiday Inn to get some much-needed rest. As he sat in the room pondering the spiritual issues gripping a shaken and divided America, a brilliant light suddenly filled the room. In the midst of the light, Jesus Christ appeared. Dressed in a luminous white robe, the risen Christ stretched out His arms toward John, who stared in amazement. Jesus motioned to him with a gesture of gentleness and kind strength.

This was the beginning of a profound change in John Michael Talbot's life and work. A short time later, an evangelical friend gave him a book about Francis of Assisi, in which he discovered the balanced, gentle life he wanted to follow. John was on his way to a new perspective and understanding. He, too, had found insight.

Reflecting later on his personal encounter with the risen Christ, he wrote:

> There is an answer to our soul's every longing. That the dream of inner and outer peace isn't an illusion. And that the potential person that God created us to be needn't remain lost and unrealized.[1]

John Michael Talbot's witness assures us that the resurrection has the power to lead us through chaotic and confusing times.

Fresh Understanding for the Body

As my own ministry unfolded through the years, I recognized that something more powerful was needed in our worship services to bring people into an encounter with the risen Christ. I had observed the revival-style method of evangelism that often turned into emotional manipulation, and I didn't want to be part of such an experience. During the late '60s, I worked with the Billy Graham team in Denver, Colorado, and found that time to be exhilarating—but I certainly wasn't Dr. Graham, and I didn't want to emulate someone else. I sensed that what was needed was something that could happen within the context of the average congregation on a regular Sunday morning. It had to be something that resonated with the average church member's experience of daily life. Bursts of emotion or whipped-up enthusiasm wouldn't fill the bill. I needed to discover a new approach filled with ancient meaning.

As I prayed about the problem, I began to sense that the answer was under my nose. Could it be that Holy Communion might be filled with profound insight that I was missing? During my seminary career, I had studied the debates that evolved through the centuries over the meaning of Communion. Prior to the Protestant Reformation in the fifteenth century, the Christian world believed that in some mystical way, the risen Christ literally extended Himself to the faithful when they received the Sacrament of the Host—that is, Communion. This notion was at the heart of the Christian faith all the way back to the Jerusalem Church under the leadership of St. James (the brother or cousin of Jesus, depending on your religious viewpoint) in A.D. 70, just before the Romans razed the city.

Once the Reformation exploded, Roman Catholics opted for a definition of Holy Communion in physical terms, maintaining that the important ingredient was the actual physical presence of Christ. Martin Luther preached against this

"There is an answer to our soul's every longing. That the dream of inner and outer peace isn't an illusion. And that the potential person that God created us to be needn't remain lost and unrealized."

—John Michael Talbot

emphasis and said that Christ was not *physically* present in Holy Communion, but instead was present the way heat fills a red-hot poker in the fireplace. In England, the Anglican Church avoided the hard-line extremes of both Luther and the Catholics. Called "the Real Presence," the Anglicans held a high view of Communion and the spiritual reality of Christ's presence in it. When the Methodist movement broke away from the Church of England, the Methodists tended to side with the Lutheran position. Along the way, Anabaptist believers concluded that Communion was nothing more that a memorial, a remembrance of Christ's dying for sin.

No one seemed to agree about much of anything.

The impact these violent disagreements had on the general public created in the average person a disinterest in Christianity and indifference to the Church. Folks who grew up in one of these traditions tended to take that church's position, but the man-on-the-street walked on by, avoiding religious quarrelling that didn't seem to have any bearing on real life. I pastored a church filled with people who fell into this latter category, and while I was glad that Communion was not a source of conflict and infighting in the congregation, I couldn't shake the feeling that this ancient ritual of the Church could offer a deeper encounter with Christ if only we could see it in a fresh way.

With people like John Michael Talbot and Don Johnson in mind, I wondered if I could find a more compelling path.

I went back to the earliest Gospel and began to rethink the teachings of Jesus. That night, gathered with His disciples for the Passover meal, He said, "Take; this is my body. . . . This is my blood of the covenant, which is poured out for many" (Mark 14:22-24).

Shoving the old theological debates aside, I asked myself what Jesus was saying in this, His original teaching. Obviously, this was only hours before His death, at the culmination of His earthly ministry. It had to be of crowning importance. Certainly, the Passover event had always been central to Jews, and Matthew's Gospel adds an important caveat to this effect: "This is my blood of the covenant, which is poured out for many for the forgiveness of sins" (26:28).

Three things seemed clear to me: The ritual instituted by Jesus that night is (1) a covenant meal (2) in which He is truly present and (3) His presence means that sins are forgiven. The covenant meal means that when people participate in it, they are entering into a relationship with God. The presence of Jesus means that He ensures the permanence of the pact, and that sin cannot subvert it.

Luke seems to agree with this understanding, and John's Gospel adds a context of extraordinary love: "If you abide in me, and my words abide in you, ask whatever you will and it shall be done for you" (15:7). I was left breathless at this promise of awesome proportions! Yet I struggled to recover the simplicity of Jesus standing before the Apostles at the Last Supper without ignoring the important ecclesial and liturgical framework that had developed over 2,000 years of Church history. What was the next step?

Looking across the sweep of Christian tradition and history, it seemed to me that the Early Church had a profound sense of reverence during Holy Communion. While I couldn't find explicit biblical evidence that they knelt when celebrating the Eucharist, it seemed to me that because kneeling requires people to humble themselves and bend low in an unusual position, they may have done so. I decided that kneeling might be a good place to start in our congregation, as well.

In the Early Church, there was a significant amount of singing in the worship services in a way that most modern congregations aren't used to. The earliest Christian services were closely related to the prayer and praise gatherings in local synagogues, and these were largely sung. What began in the synagogues and was passed on to the New Testament Church is now preserved in what is called "Gregorian chant." In the fifth century, Pope Gregory saved this Hebrew form of music from extinction, and it continued to be used throughout the Middle Ages. I thought that this musical form might help our church to cultivate both a reverence and an openness to the presence of Christ.

The Gospels' use of the Greek word *oinos* makes it clear that early believers used wine, not grape juice. After some consideration, I felt that we could have both options available for anyone who might have a problem with fermented juice.

Scripture is also clear that Jesus used a common cup and a single loaf of unleavened bread. Rather than drinking out of their own individual cups, the Apostles had passed around the "cup of the covenant" that Jesus had blessed. This sharing conveyed unity. I felt this was an important element to incorporate into our service, particularly for believers who had not come out of our denomination's tradition. Ideally, a ritual is a starting point for reality: If we enacted this symbol of our oneness, it could help us learn to *be* one.

The resurrection opened the door for the presence of Jesus to convey divine insight, and this is one of the many reasons that it remains the central conviction in the Christian faith.

Chapter 8

Studying various liturgies of the Church from both Orthodox and Roman Catholic traditions, in addition to other historic groups, I gained a sense that Early Church worship was a combination of form and spontaneity, of liturgy and creativity. The people who came to worship knew what they were doing and had a clear spiritual focus. As I surveyed the people in my congregation and considered our tradition's general lack of creative spontaneity, I felt led to guide the believers in this direction. If they could come to expect the unexpected, it wouldn't be too hard for them to believe that the risen Christ waited to meet them in the sacrament of Holy Communion.

It took some time to pull all these elements together. I had kneeling rails built. I had music personnel, thankfully, who developed moving songs and hymns for the service. And then we were ready: Leaders in the church served the bread and wine to people as they knelt at the rails. I kept talking in the background, suggesting from Scripture what the participants might expect and should seek as they received the Eucharist.

For each service, I chose a theme that I emphasized during the Scripture lessons and the sermon and in my remarks as people came down the aisle to receive Communion. While the themes varied, I kept in view the goal of bringing believers into a personal experience with the risen Christ.

In a short time, the Communion service became one of the most important events in our congregation's life. After one service, I was standing at the back shaking hands when a man I had never seen before came through the greeting line. I always

110

tried to give visitors a special welcome and learn something about them. When I asked him about himself, his response stopped me in my tracks.

"I've always wanted to meet Jesus Christ," the man announced. "Today I did."

"I don't understand," I said.

"I've wanted to have a personal encounter for a long time," he said. "You showed me how to find one."

"I don't think I'm getting you," I replied. "Today was a Communion service."

"Oh, yes. That's where it happened. You told us to envision Jesus Christ entering our lives as we received the elements. You said that He would come into us just as the bread and wine are absorbed into our bodies. I told Jesus I wanted to see His face and that's when it happened."

Long after the man had gone home, I tried to understand why I was so surprised. *Wasn't this exactly what I wanted to occur?* Except . . . it happened so easily! This kind of meeting with Christ was what I had hoped for and intended, yet I was still left with my mouth hanging open in astonishment.

On another occasion, a woman struggling with cancer came to see me several months after one of the special Eucharist services. As she sat in my office and told her story, I was once again surprised and amazed.

"I knew something had happened that Sunday," she began. "It occurred during the moments when I was receiving Communion, but I didn't want to mention it until I'd gone back to the doctor for at least two months in a row."

"What happened during Communion time?" I murmured.

"My physician is delighted because the cancer has gone into remission," she continued with a broad smile. "He's not sure why, but I know. I told him that I had a healing experience during the Sunday morning service. I felt the moment it happened."

Healing during a Communion service? But what else would we expect when the risen Christ appears?

These are just two of many people who have knelt at the Communion rail and met the resurrected Lord. As I sought a fresh understanding for how to lead believers to encounter Him, it was the risen One who gave me the insight! The resurrection opened the door for the presence of Jesus to convey divine insight, and this is one of the many reasons that it remains the central conviction in the Christian faith.

Note
1. John Michael Talbot with Steve Rabey, *The Lessons of St. Francis* (New York: Penguin Group, 1998), p. 13.

CHAPTER 9

Receptivity

With the summer approaching, I needed to take my lawn mower down to the repair shop in Evergreen, Colorado. I loaded the heavy machine in the back of my jeep and drove from our mountain home down the highway to the little town. As I was unloading the mower, the repairman noticed that the license tag on my Jeep was from Oklahoma, and asked why I had an out-of-state plate. I explained that my wife Margueritte and I had two homes, one in Colorado and one in Oklahoma.

"Lived there once," the man said.

"Really?"

"Yeah," the man said. "In Muskogee. Everybody in that town tried to save my soul."

"Did they succeed?" I asked.

"Not on your life," the repairman grumbled. "I was able to fight them off."

I thought about this conversation later. Some people have the spiritual sensitivity of my lawn mower, while others carry a burning intensity to have a relationship with God. One has the switch turned to On; the other doesn't even know there is a switch.

Often during the college years or on their first job, young people develop an intense spiritual interest. But if nothing happens to fan the spark into flame, they may run the rat race for decades before their spiritual needs catch up with them and they again become aware of their emptiness. During the late middle years, a new spiritual openness can start to simmer—but if nothing occurs to make spiritual awareness come to a full boil, connection with God may slide away and not reappear again for a long time. Old age often finds people who have reached the conclusion that their life is already spent—they missed their chance at spiritual fulfillment. They'll have to live with emptiness until they fill a grave.

But it's just not true. An encounter with Jesus can resurrect the atrophied muscles of spiritual sensitivity at any time, at any age—if we are open to the unexpected.

Sensitive to the Unexpected

On a cold, rainy night, Ramona Hanson, an attorney in Edmond, Oklahoma, looked in her kitchen cabinet and was startled to realize that she needed to run down to the local quick-stop grocery story—a place she usually didn't shop. The convenience store was located near a cemetery close to Boulevard and Danforth streets. The rain came straight down, unabated. As she pulled into the parking lot, a man appeared directly in the path of her car. Ramona slammed on the brakes and stared at the figure caught in her car's headlights.

It was anything but a good night to be out on the street without an umbrella. Slouched against the downpour, the man had the ragged appearance of a homeless drifter. He seemed to be counting a few coins in a shaking hand.

From out of nowhere, Ramona felt a strong urge to give the man some help. For no particular reason, she felt it was crucial to offer some money before this moment disappeared. Reaching into her purse, Ramona pulled out two $20 bills and jumped out of the car. Running through the rain, she approached the stooped man.

"Here," Ramona said. "This is for you." Then she turned around and started running back through the rain.

"I love you, lady," the stranger called out.

Ramona jumped in the car and wanted to yell out the window, "I love you, too . . . and I always have!" But she didn't. She had no idea why she'd even consider saying such a thing to a complete stranger.

Putting the car in gear, Ramona Hanson drove toward home, her errand forgotten. As she contemplated what had just happened, Romana recognized that her behavior had been totally out of character.

Suddenly a profound awareness gripped her: The man was Jesus. The Lord had wanted to tell her she was loved.

Whipping the car around, Ramona hurried back to the quick stop. She felt guilty that she hadn't given Him everything in her purse, or maybe offered a ride! But when she reached the grocery shop, the man had vanished. She sat in her car silently, pondering her encounter. Ramona knew that she had met the risen Christ.

The earliest life of the Christian Church was sustained by encounters such as Ramona's. With their backs to the wall, facing savage persecution from the Roman government, the first believers knew the meaning of hardship. However difficult life

An encounter with Jesus can
resurrect the atrophied muscles of
spiritual sensitivity at any time,
at any age—if we are open
to the unexpected.

became, however, the first believers refused to allow persecution to make them calloused, to harden their sensitivity to God.

As the New Testament ends, we find the apostle John marooned on the Isle of Patmos. The Roman emperor had brought his hammer down with a savage blow on all who followed Christ, and the pressure would not let up for two centuries. Death in the arenas continued as gentle men and women were fed to the lions. Against this backdrop, John had the extraordinary visions that would become the book of Revelation.

A voice commanded the apostle to write, and a menorah with seven candlesticks appeared before him. Among the flames, an extraordinary figure appeared with eyes like fire and hair as white as snow (see Rev. 1:12-20). Because the Roman soldiers were everywhere watching, John had to write in veiled terms, so he called the figure "son of man," a term that Jesus used to describe Himself, from the book of Daniel. According to John, the Son of Man held seven stars in His right hand, and a double-edged sword came out of His mouth. The rest of the revelation continues with similar imagery.

Is the experience of Ramona Hanson any stranger than what John described? Most people would probably find Ramona's experience *less* bizarre.

In any case, what the first-century apostle John and the twenty-first-century disciple Ramona had in common was a receptivity to the Spirit of Jesus.

The Gift of a Brush with Death

During my seminary years, I attended a highly academic graduate school where doubt was encouraged. It was not unusual for students to fight over questions about the resurrection in the classroom and halls. One particular student was unusually bright and talented, but refused to accept Jesus as any more than a humanist of the highest order. A physically big guy, John Schmidt certainly respected the Christian story, but he functioned like a humanist or a Unitarian who didn't believe God intervened in history and concluded that the resurrection accounts were only expressions of ancient myth-making. John and I had many heated arguments. When he graduated, I didn't expect to see John again.

A couple decades later, I was ministering Holy Communion in a large conference held by Dr. Francis McNutt. A former Roman Catholic priest, Francis had a phenomenal healing ministry that extended around the world. Around this massive auditorium, Protestant and Orthodox ministers were holding Communion Services while Roman Catholics did the same. I prepared to administer the sacrament, and when I looked up— there stood John Schmidt.

I nearly dropped the chalice. *What is John Schmidt doing at an event designed to teach people how to continue the healing ministry of Jesus Christ?* As large as ever, John smiled, winked and took Communion. After the service, he waited to talk to me.

"What are you doing here?" I asked in amazement.

"My ideas have changed," John said modestly.

"How?" I pressed.

"I went to Vietnam as a military chaplain. They sent me out to the front lines, where I crawled through the muck and mud to reach dying men. All around me, I found soldiers with their arms and legs blown off. Lying in foxholes with terrified young men, I realized I had nothing to tell them. My seminary faith was bankrupt. I had to find out if Jesus the Christ was really alive." He smiled. "I did. He is."

As I stood there listening to this good man, I realized that his life had been profoundly touched by the risen Christ. In his own way, John Schmidt now had a resurrection story to tell. What had cut through the noise and doubts and allowed him to be receptive? The reality of death! The experience of coming face to face with darkness had brought John to the Light.

A personal encounter with death has a unique way of planting in us a new seed of spiritual sensitivity. The transitory concerns of daily life disappear when we look death in the eye.

Receptive to *Whom?*

In the third century, the Roman emperor Constantine needed political support and national unity, and he hoped Christianity would foot the bill. While his motives remain unclear and the legitimacy of his personal faith questionable, Constantine summoned the Council of Nicea, calling on Christian leaders to present a singular statement of their beliefs and convictions.

For at least a century before Nicea, Christians had used the Apostles Creed to define and protect the faith handed down from the Apostles:

> I believe in God the Father Almighty, Creator of heaven and earth, and in Jesus Christ His only Son, our Lord: Who was conceived of the Holy Spirit, born of the Virgin Mary, suffered under Pontius Pilate, was crucified, died and was buried . . .

Let's be clear about what happened

when Jesus Christ stepped out of

the tomb. It was not reanimation

or resuscitation. It was new life.

The embodied, risen Christ became

timeless, never again to die.

From Constantine's assembly came the Nicene Creed, which defines who Jesus Christ was in terms that shifted from a Hebrew worldview to a Greek perspective—that is, from a personal statement of faith to be made in community with other believers ("I believe") to a universal presentation of belief to those outside the faith community ("We believe"):

> We believe in one Lord, Jesus Christ, the only Son of God, eternally begotten of the Father, God from God, Light from Light, true God from true God, begotten, not made, of one Being with the Father . . .

For this statement, the word "begotten" was carefully chosen. Its implication is that Jesus was *of like kind* to the Father. God can only beget God, in the same way people can only beget people, not cats or kangaroos. The Creed was meant to conclusively settle the matter of the divinity of Jesus.

The third major statement of the Church's faith appeared sometime in the fourth or fifth century in the Athanasian Creed, which declares:

> We worship one God in trinity and the Trinity in unity, neither confusing the Persons nor dividing the divine Being. For the Father is one Person, the Son is another, and the Spirit is still another. But the deity of the Father, Son and Holy Spirit is one, equal in glory, coeternal in majesty. . . .

It's important to note that the Church went to great lengths to remain monotheistic while proclaiming that the fullness of God had come in Jesus and that the Holy Spirit is the personality of Jesus let loose in the world. (We would do well to remember this, living in a time when the work of the Holy Spirit is preeminently emphasized. As believers talk about wonderful expressions of power and gifting, they sometimes make it sound like the Holy Spirit is a god unto Himself. We must stay in touch with the fact that these signs and wonders are the work of the Spirit of the risen Christ.)

The bottom line? Christians made sure the world knew three things:

1. Believers are monotheists, because there is only one God.
2. Jesus was absolutely and completely a man.
3. Jesus was absolutely and completely divine.

How was this possible? Well, that's the mystery. Fully human, Jesus was also the fullness of God the Father. Of course, the ancient world turned up its nose at the idea. For Jews, God clothing Himself in flesh was unthinkable, even blasphemous. For Greco-Romans, it didn't really matter—their myriad gods took on human form all the time. Christians, however, clung to the notion that the one God had vested Himself in Jesus. This indwelling is what made it possible for Jesus to rise from the dead with a new physical body that was somehow different from the one in which He died.

Let's be clear about what happened when Jesus Christ stepped out of the tomb. It was not reanimation or resuscitation. It was *new life*. To understand the difference, consider how the raising of Lazarus was different from the resurrection of Jesus. Lazarus was reanimated; Jesus was resurrected. Lazarus was restored only to die later. The embodied, risen Christ became timeless, never again to die.

It is this Lord's Spirit who tunes our souls to receive His guidance, His nudges toward deeper spiritual connection.

Wholeness

Mark's Gospel begins his account of Jesus' ministry with the outline of a sermon. Jesus came into the area surrounding the Lake of Galilee with a singular message: "The time is fulfilled, and the kingdom of God is a hand."

Matthew elaborates on the content of Jesus' ministry: "He went about all Galilee, teaching in their synagogues and preaching the gospel of the kingdom and healing every disease and every infirmity among the people. So his fame spread throughout all Syria, and they brought him all the sick, those afflicted with various diseases and pains, demoniacs, epileptics, and paralytics, and he healed them" (4:23-24).

According to Mark and Matthew, Jesus' ministry had three dimensions: *teaching*, *preaching* and *healing*—all performed with extraordinary results.

According to the book of Acts, the ministry of the newborn Church had these same three dimensions. The same work of teaching, preaching and healing continued, even after Jesus' ascension, with equally amazing results.

On the Day of Pentecost, Peter *preached* and 3,000 people joined the Church (see Acts 2:1-41).

Shortly after that event, Peter and John were going up to the Temple and encountered a 40-year-old beggar who was lame from birth. They commanded him to walk in the name of Jesus. The man was immediately *healed* (see Acts 3:1-10).

After a crowd gathered because of this amazing miracle, Peter and John held a *teaching* session so powerful that it got them thrown in jail (see Acts 3:11-26). When they were brought to trial, Peter boldly proclaimed, "There is no other name under heaven given among men by which we must be saved" (Acts 4:12).

The leaders of the Sanhedrin became afraid when they saw how the people praised God for what had happened, and they released Peter and John.

Not a bad couple of days!

Over the centuries, the ministry of healing seems to have diminished some in the Church, but it has never completely ceased. Having lost the ability to use the gift of healing, some Reformers in the fifteenth century declared that healing ministry ended at the close of the first century. Their reactionary response proved premature, however, and even today the ministry endures.

In recent decades, healing has sometimes come to be called *wholeness*. This is in recognition that disease and disorder must not be considered only in physical terms—they involve mental, emotional and social factors as well. The kingdom of God extends the redemptive, healing work of the Creator across the entire planet, bringing renewal to everything from mental illness to systemic poverty, from broken families to deadly viruses. "Wholeness" is a bigger word, a word that captures the worldwide deliverance that occurs through an encounter with the loving power of God.

Does It Still Happen?

Absolutely. Throughout the five decade span of my own ministry, I've observed the phenomenon of healing occurring many times. Of course, healing prayer cannot be handled with the orderliness and predictability of preaching a weekly sermon or teaching a Sunday School lesson, but the restorative ministry of the kingdom of God continues to be poured out on people week after week.

For over a decade, I've been on the board of directors for Francis McNutt's healing ministry. Formerly a Roman Catholic priest before marrying his wife, Judith, Francis worked around the world before he established a healing center in Jacksonville, Florida. Through the years with Francis, I've observed and seen many people touched and restored.

My friend has made efforts to chronicle, in a scientific fashion, what happens when people are prayed for. In one of these experiments, Francis took a team of people into a local hospital to test the difference between arthritic sufferers who were prayed for and those who were not. A camera recorded what happened as people received prayer. At the end of the film, the patients' doctor explains how the recovery rate of those who were prayed for was significantly better than the other group. In the middle of his explanation, the doctor is so overwhelmed by the evidence that she breaks into tears. The evidence is *that* compelling.

Yes, healing still happens!

And here's an example: Raised in a Christian home, Dale Howard was a bright 10-year-old child who suffered a chronic sinus condition. His nasal passages would close up at night,

Disease and disorder must not be considered only in physical terms— they involve mental, emotional and social factors as well. The kingdom of God extends the redemptive, healing work of the Creator across the entire planet, bringing renewal to everything from mental illness to systemic poverty, from broken families to deadly viruses.

making it difficult for him to sleep. During very severe bouts, Dale would remain home from school, suffering with debilitating headaches. Various medicines, prescribed through his many trips to the doctor, offered some relief, but certainly didn't cure his problem.

In October 1963, Dale's mother made him attend a revival service at Grace Trinity Church, because his father was out of town and couldn't watch him while she went to the service. Dale had homework assignments that had to be done, however, and after a give-and-take argument, his mother agreed that he could sit on the back row of the church to do his homework during the worship service. Unfortunately, his fidgeting made so much noise that his mother eventually made Dale come up and sit by her near the front.

At the end of the evening, the young evangelist called people to come forward for prayer, and Dale's mother was convinced it would be good for him. To avoid arguing with her, he stood on the outside of the circle of people while the evangelist prayed for others. Finally Dale's turn came.

As the evangelist laid his hands on Dale, the man stopped and said loudly, "This young man has faith!" Fervent prayer began again.

Suddenly, all thoughts of homework were pushed aside and Dale was aware of an unseen Presence standing in front of him. The awareness increased until he couldn't deny that he was standing before Jesus Christ.

Tears began to stream down his face. Never in his life had he been in the presence of anyone who seemed so *real*, even though no one else could see Him. Dale's weeping continued and his sense of amazement grew. Tears of joy flowed down his face.

On their way home that night, Dale looked out the window of the car at the houses and streets in the old part of town. Turning to his mother, he said confidently, "Everything is brand-new." Of course it wasn't, but Dale had been made new and the world looked different.

Later that evening, Dale sat at the table with his mother, eating a Little Debbie cream cake and talking about their evening. Suddenly he realized that he could breathe.

"What's happened to you?" Dale's mother asked.

With astonishment in his voice, Dale said, "I think . . . I think I've been . . . healed!"

Dale's sinus condition was gone! And it never came back. He was well. His encounter with the risen Christ brought such a depth of newness that his body was revitalized.

An Early History

Trying to make sense out of these stories is challenging because they occur on the border between matter and energy, in the shadowy realm between the known and the unknown. For 2,000 years, believers have wandered in and out of this mystery and not always understood where they were going. However bumbling their efforts, one of the most extraordinary results has been the continuation through the centuries of Jesus' healing ministry through the Church.

Over time, the Roman Catholic Church began to view ministries of healing as the province of saints, as if those who performed them had special capabilities and everyone else need not worry about praying for the sick. The message of this ecclesiastical ladder seemed to be that the regular membership of the Church shouldn't expect results from their prayers. Unfortunately, restoration came to be seen as the exception rather than the rule.

The earliest Church functioned under a completely different set of assumptions. Believing that baptism symbolized a very real going down into death with Christ and coming up into the newness of the resurrection, the members of the Early Church expected healing power to flow into them, and through them to the sick. They identified with the resurrection to such a degree that they entered into the gifts and empowerments that the risen Lord imparted. They assumed that a newly baptized believer would receive gifts, including healing.

Tertullian, a Church Father in the second century, told the newly baptized to come out of the waters with their arms wide open to receive the charism (the gifts of the Spirit).[1] A century later, Cyril of Jerusalem described the wide range of believers who could receive these same gifts.[2] The earliest Christian writers included such extraordinary figures as St. Hilary of Poitiers and St. John Chrysotom, both of whom believed that immediately after baptism gifts of empowerment would be imparted.[3]

In our time, baptism has come to be seen more like a bar mitzvah, a crossing of the line into adolescence—nothing more than the fulfillment of a ritual demand. Believers often come with no expectation of anything happening other than getting wet. Some of our contemporary problems stem from this way of thinking. In contrast, Origen, the extraordinary Church Father martyred around 253, anticipated that all Christians would have amazing capacities that included healing gifts.[4]

One of the greatest medieval leaders of the Church, Bernard of Clairvaux, was the most significant religious force of his age. In 1115, Bernard founded the Cistercian monastery at Clairvaux and began to preach the mystic contemplation of Christ as his highest spiritual joy. During his life he restored unity to the Church and brought healing to the people.[5] This same pattern continued over and over through the centuries with leaders like St. Francis Xavier and John Wesley.[6] Ministries that proclaimed the resurrection with forceful insight could expect outpourings of healing and wholeness. The healing ministry of Christ never stopped.

One of the most remarkable healing ministries began at Lourdes, France, in the life of a young girl named Bernadette. Because of the role of the Virgin Mary in Bernadette's story, Protestants have tended to discount her witness. Nevertheless, one of the most extraordinary healing centers in the world still thrives around her grotto. The Medical Bureau at Lourdes is maintained with scientific personnel who document the healing events that occur and measure them against a strictly controlled standard. The data confirms that the sick have been made whole in Lourdes for more than 150 years.[7]

Why is that such a surprise to us? Because the people of the twenty-first century flounder in the backwash of the Enlightenment, which led to an emphasis on facts over faith. No shadowy realm here! Factual evidence has become the prerequisite to venturing into the world of the mystical and unseen. We have adopted a closed-mindedness to anything that doesn't come out of a computer or a calculator. The average person tends to accept the idea that if you can't see it, *it* isn't! The "thing" doesn't exist. (Never mind atoms, wind, germs, love, trust or hope—none of which can be seen with the human eye.) We've become basic, factual folks who stick with the tangible, resulting in an internal blindness that limits our observations of any event that is outside the realm of science—such as the resurrection.

Yet God seems to be healing in miraculous ways in inverse proportion to our closed-mindedness. An extremely high number of healing incidences have occurred in the last 100 years, as if God has been attempting to jar our senses into an awareness of the risen Christ. This phenomenon is opposite to what we see in earlier centuries. In times gone by, the resurrected Lord appeared and people were healed as a consequence of His appearance. Now, amazing healings cause society to look for the risen Christ.

The Healing Revival

The healing revival of the 1940s and '50s shook North America. A group of preachers with tents and loud speakers proclaimed the gospel, and at the end of the services, listeners were invited to come forward to receive healing ministry. In addition to these traveling preachers, such as Jack Coe and William M. Branham, a new mode of communication—called television—broadcasted the faces of people such as Oral Roberts across America's TV screens. A child at the time, I remember sitting in front of the large set, watching Roberts surrounded by massive crowds. My family didn't approve and I didn't know what to make of it, but I watched in fascination.

Believing that baptism symbolized
a very real going down into death
with Christ and coming up into the
newness of the resurrection,
the members of the Early Church
expected healing power to flow
into them, and through them to
the sick. They assumed that a newly
baptized believer would
receive gifts, including healing.

Most of these preachers were not particularly well-educated and had come from humble beginnings, often from homes that were troubled with alcoholism or child abandonment. They were generally poor people burning with a passion for the gospel. Arising from lower-class surroundings, they were cut off from the usual college opportunities of the professional clergy, but they were also liberated from the intellectual struggles running rampant on university campuses.

What started small exploded with vigor across the American scene. William Branham grew up in a dirt floor log cabin in the backwoods of Kentucky and became a major leader in healing ministry. Even after reaching national prominence, Branham dressed in cheap clothing—his humble beginning imparted a humility to Branham that served him well during his nationwide ministry. Unfortunately, his poor background also meant that he was naive about finances, and he had income tax problems that severely affected his work, as well as theological ideas that reflected his lack of education. Still, his ministry touched multitudes.

Oral Roberts burst on the scene in the late '40s and early '50s with a mystique that spellbound the masses. Probably the most popular of all the healing evangelists, Roberts also proved to be one of the most capable. At the touch of his hand, the worst of diseases vanished. While various types of controversy occasionally followed him, he was a respectable face for the Pentecostals—because he kept accountability with his funds, he was seen in a positive light. The development of Oral Roberts University added a stature that still endures. Possibly more than any other person, Oral Roberts brought healing ministry to a new and respectable forefront in the life of American mainstream churches.

Along with Branham and Roberts, men like Jack Coe and A. A. Allen touched multitudes. T. L. Osborn spoke to millions and particularly carried the respect of the mainstream church. He preached in more than 80 nations and his writings were published in 130 languages and dialects.

The list could go on and on with the names of people who worked their way across America, preaching, teaching and healing. The wide impact of these ministries accelerated the acceptance of healing prayer and work in the evangelical church, while the ministries of Father D'Orio and Padre Pio had the same result in the Roman Catholic Church. Shifting toward the label "wholeness" rather than "healing" enabled many to affirm this ministry of the Church outside of a Pentecostal context.

Modern Doubts

In 1914, an entire congregation in Wales saw a vision of the resurrected Jesus. Stephen Jeffreys, a coal miner, had become something of an amazing preacher and started the church. Ten years before, when he was 28, a revival touched large numbers of people throughout the country.

When the vision occurred, Jeffreys and the entire congregation experienced the appearance for a full six hours. For three days, Jeffreys was so overwhelmed that he lay on the floor. The experience resulted in an astonishing empowerment for healing work.[8]

What followed became a ministry that touched multitudes. Deaf ears suddenly began to hear and blind eyes to see. Physical restorations happened continually, with people leaving wheel-chairs behind. Polio victims with "irreparable damage" started walking again. Jeffreys was particularly able to bring whole-ness to people suffering with rheumatoid arthritis. Reports tell of bones loudly popping as the body relocated itself during the meetings.

Why haven't you heard of this phenomenon? In the 1920s, U.S. newspapers didn't print much news from Wales. For America, that was way off the beaten track. And there was another reason.

Mainstream churches and the secular public considered such reports nonsense or examples of religious extremism. Many groups like Jeffreys's church were of a Pentecostal per-suasion, and in those days such congregations were considered to be expressions of mob emotionalism. Middle- and upper-class folks believed that poor people were acting out their pent-up anger and unresolved issues.

During my childhood, my friends and I heard that just such a Pentecostal church had started out on the edge of town. The " 'postolics" or "holy rollers" were talked about with fasci-nated interest by my parents' friends. When I heard that the Pentecostals were only a notch above the crazies, I had to know what was going on. The rumors of extremism would have fas-cinated any already-overactive young boy.

Several of my friends and I spent an evening creeping up on the church, like soldiers positioning for a sneak attack. Once we got under the building's windows, we could hear a considerable amount of shouting, wailing, sobbing and laugh-ing inside. We imagined wild people screaming and going into gyrations. If you listened to our stories later, you'd have thought we had gone to the circus. In fact, we saw nothing—if we had seen broken people crying and being offered comfort, it would probably have scared us to death. Being overcome by God was a foreign and suspicious concept in our town.

And not just in our town. In the early 1900s, John G. Lake began a healing ministry in Spokane, Washington, that is documented to have produced more than 100,000 healings and miracles in the first five years of its existence.[9] Have you heard of this ministry? I thought not.

It is likely that his difficult family background strongly influenced Lake's interest in healing ministry. Born in Ontario, Canada, he had grown up in a family where illness seemed to be the norm. Eight of his siblings died from digestive disorders. Another sister died of cancer and a brother was an invalid for 22 years. John Lake's wife had both tuberculosis and heart disease. Lake himself struggled with rheumatism that had distorted his leg.

While pastoring a Methodist Church in Wisconsin, his problem pushed him into a prayer experience in Chicago, during which his leg miraculously straightened under the ministry of John Dowie. Dowie had started "healing homes," and when Lake brought his brother and sister, they were also instantly healed.

John Lake's life and ministry were revolutionary. After a stint of powerful healing work in South Africa, he returned to Spokane and started his ministry there. The healing ministry became so powerful and extraordinary that he was endorsed by the mayor of Spokane and the Queen of the Netherlands. Many good church members today would find the stories of Lake's ministry hard to believe—if they ever heard the stories.

Why haven't you heard of him? The bias of the times. Newspapers and magazines aim at the American mainstream. Even major Christian denominations target middle-of-the-road America because it's easier to cater to the middle than it is to challenge it. When happenings run against the current of the majority's philosophical and religious ideas, you don't hear much about the John Lakes of recent history.

I know. I've been there.

Following a divine intervention that saved my life from a deadly kidney disease when I was 29, I started studying healing ministry and talked with people such as Oral Roberts and Kathryn Khulman. I'd grown up knowing of Roberts, but knew nothing about Khulman at that time. After months of gathering data, I announced to my congregation that in a month we would have a healing service on Sunday night. Actually, I decided to try such a service more as an act of faith than anything else. Because I was always trying out innovative ideas on the congregation, I think most people assumed the service was a play on words of some sort. Not many of the members really took me seriously. As the evening approached, I began to grow increasingly afraid. *What if nothing happened? I'd look like a fool!* By the time of the announced Sunday night, I was a nervous wreck.

Wearing a sober black clerical robe to avoid any appearance of emotionalism, I walked down the center aisle and was surprised to see the number that had attended. I got to the front, and we began.

The first half of the service was so high church that it would have almost given you a nose-bleed. Truth is, I was marking time, trying to avoid praying for people as long as possible. When the time finally came and they began coming forward, I was terrified. But I started down the row of kneeling people and put my hands on their heads, praying for each one. Nothing much happened, which to me was somewhat of a relief.

But then I came to a dear lady who was something of a spiritual mother to me. I knew that she had received a medical diagnosis of deteriorating ankles and would soon be confined to a wheelchair for the rest of her life. As I laid my hands on her head, the prayer time became electric, so powerful that I almost forgot what I was doing.

Sure enough, a week later the doctors confirmed that she had been restored to complete wholeness.

But here's the kicker: I didn't know how to talk about the healings. Pastor friends didn't want to discuss the experience, and most of the people in the church looked the other way because they had no way to explain what had happened in natural terms. With some of my clerical associates, I was marginalized for attempting that type of ministry. Even if sick people were restored to wholeness, laying hands on people in the '60s and '70s was considered too extreme in my mainline denomination.

There's nothing abnormal about these reactions. It's human nature to turn our eyes away when circumstances are too unsettling. Isn't that what Jesus' closest associates did at the sight of the empty tomb on Easter morning?

God is still using healing

ministry to confront a doubting public

with the reality of the risen Christ.

While many people begin praying

for the sick because of an encounter

with the risen Lord, many others

encounter Jesus because they've

had a healing experience.

The Bottom Line

God is still using healing ministry to confront a doubting public with the reality of the risen Christ. While many people begin praying for the sick because of an encounter with the risen Lord, many others encounter Jesus *because* they have had a healing experience.

Can this be proved or demonstrated? No, it can't. Our culture says that once something has been confirmed scientifically, then we can believe it. The world of faith, however, operates on the opposite system—which is logical in its own way. First, you act on your convictions and then God confirms the truth of them. As St. Augustine put it succinctly: "I believe and therefore I know."

Finding the reality of the risen Christ begins by reaching out in conviction and trust. The abundance of healing miracles in our time tells us that's still a promise. The resurrection has made it so.

Notes

1. Killian McDonnell and George T. Montague, *Fanning the Flames: What Does Baptism in the Holy Spirit Have to Do with Christian Initiation?* (Collegeville, MN: Liturgical Press, 1991), p. 16.
2. Ibid., p. 23.
3. Williston Walker, *A History of the Christian Church* (New York: Charles Scribner's Sons, 1959), pp. 225-226.
4. Dr. Lester Sumrall, *Pioneers of Faith* (South Bend, IN: Sumrall Publishing, 1995), p. 92.
5. John Crowder, *Miracle Workers, Reformers, and the New Mystics* (Shippensburg, PA: Destiny Image Publishers, 2006), p. 286.
6. Ibid., pp. 287-290.
7. Ibid., pp. 323-333.
8. David Edwin Harrell, Jr., *All Things Are Possible: The Healing and Charismatic Revivals in Modern America* (Bloomington, IN: Indiana University Press, 1978), p. 64.
9. Crowder, *Miracle Workers, Reformers, and the New Mystics*, pp. 289-290.

Hope

Early on Easter 1983, Rev. Mike Owen was preparing for the 8 A.M. Sunday service. As Easter always is in Oklahoma, spring was breaking out with new flowers and the bright green of the budding trees and returning grass, signaling new life bursting forth everywhere. Bowing his head at the altar rail, Mike prayed fervently, thanking God for the death of Christ that brought salvation for our sin and renewal of our lives. Mike particularly praised God for the resurrection, and how the raising of Jesus Christ had set us free from fear.

As Mike prayed, he became aware of an overwhelming Presence. He looked up and saw the risen Christ standing on the other side of the rail, holding out His hands. Mike stared in amazement. Before him stood a complete image of Jesus. Then Mike heard Him say, "I am alive forevermore." The figure was like a painting, but more lucid and transparent. Mike saw Him even as he was looking through Him. Abruptly, Jesus disappeared.

Mike Owen didn't need anything about his faith confirmed. He believed in the Lord, the Bible, the resurrection—everything that comprises the Christian faith. Instead, the experience came in the context of thanking God for all that he already accepted. Yet the encounter did take Mike to a deeper level of conviction, a degree of assurance that he hadn't even known existed. Sometime in the past, Mike had heard an old preacher say, "I know deeper in my knower," and that phrase rang true for him on that Easter morning. In no way did he doubt the resurrection, but a more profound awareness arose out of this moment of worship.

Even though Mike Owen is a preacher to this day, he doesn't often share this story. He believes that members of the congregation should base their faith on what they find in the Scripture, not on his experience. Nevertheless, that moment remains a monumental landmark in his journey, giving birth to a new assurance of enduring hope.

A New Assurance

Contemporary Judaism flows from the hand and work of Rabbi Jochanan ben Zakkai. The brilliant rabbi was carried out of Jerusalem by stealth during the destruction of the city in A.D. 70. Ben Zakkai climbed into a wooden coffin and his followers put in a putrefying piece of a leg to deter the Romans from checking to see if he was inside. In this way, ben Zakkai was smuggled through the city's gates.[1]

Rabbi ben Zakkai was one of the few who survived the total annihilation of the ancient city. Setting up a new center of work near Galilee, the rabbi began the difficult task of rebuilding a decimated way of life. Replacing the sacrificial system of Jerusalem's Temple—which was no longer possible—with the study of the Torah, ben Zakkai radically reinterpreted Judaism. The rabbi's work was so impressive that his disciples called him the "strong hammer" and the "lamp of Israel."

As death approached, however, dark shadows fell over ben Zakkai. His followers discovered him weeping on his deathbed. When asked why he struggled and exhibited such grief, ben Zakkai responded, "There are two ways before me, one leading to Paradise and the other to Gehinnom, and I do not know by which I shall be taken. Shall I not weep?"

Even with his highly significant contributions, this great rabbi, a contemporary of Jesus' Apostles, had no certainty that he had achieved the highest eternal reward. The same was true of Rabbi Jochanan bar Nappacha, who died in A.D. 290 after his rabbinical school produced the Jerusalem Talmud. Instead of being buried in either white or black clothing, the rabbi requested a neutral shade so that he would not offend if he was given a place among either the righteous or the sinners.[2]

Confidence based on works cannot be an assurance of reaching heaven—when works are trusted for hope in the afterlife, fear triumphs over faith. As death approached for these truly great leaders, their hope diminished. These were good men, but they would have had trouble making sense out of the apostle John's proclamation: "God gave us eternal life, and this life is in his Son. He who has the Son has life; he who has not the Son of God has not life. I write this to you who believe in the name of the Son of God, that you may know that you have eternal life" (1 John 5:11-13). Jochanan ben Zakkai and Jochanan bar Nappacha wouldn't have comprehended John's promise.

But neither would Peter, John, Andrew, James and the rest of the Apostles until after Easter morning. The resurrection of Jesus Christ made a revolutionary difference in their definition of hope. Peter boldly proclaimed:

The most significant and

powerful act of God in history

was the resurrection of Jesus Christ

from the dead. Death was

defeated and new life

released around the globe.

Blessed be the God and Father of our Lord Jesus Christ! By his great mercy we have been born anew to a living hope through the resurrection of Jesus Christ from the dead, and to an inheritance which is imperishable, undefiled, and unfading, kept in heaven for you, who by God's power are guarded through faith for a salvation ready to be revealed in the last time. In this you rejoice, though now for a little while you may have to suffer various trials (1 Pet. 1:3, *NASB*).

The contrast between Peter's daring confidence and the rabbis' fear is obvious. The resurrection made a bold difference.

Recently I wrote a book on near-death experiences, for which I interviewed Christians who had crossed the line between life and death and then returned to this world.[3] While many aspects of their stories are fascinating and confounding, one of the universal themes I discovered was the loss of their fear of dying. Those who have returned agree that the universal fear of life's end disappears once they experience what Peter calls a "living hope." Nothing is left to dread.

While many Christians take hope for granted today, it is worthwhile to remember that this hope sprang from a world rife with terror and fear. First-century people lived in an age without antiseptic or anesthesia. Because penicillin and a million other modern drugs were unknown, countless numbers died of diseases that today are virtually unremembered. Lifespan was short and infant mortality high. Poverty and warfare added to dismal expectations for the future. Obviously, it was not an easy time to be alive! Hope was important.

Chapter 11

Chesed

One of the Hebrew concepts that have constantly rung in the ears of Jewish people is that of God's continued faithfulness, kindness and mercy—*chesed* in Hebrew—to His covenant-people. He will never let Israel go. The word expresses an unearned, comprehensive love. The New Testament word that comes as close as any to encompassing this idea is translated "grace." Such forbearing love was extended to Israel through the covenant made with Abraham and renewed at Sinai with Moses. Completely unimaginable in human terms, *chesed* expresses a love that continues on to uncountable generations of Jews who know that their redemption has always been contingent on God's work on their behalf. When they were helpless, the Creator came to their aid purely because of His own choosing.

The New Testament stands as a testimony to the fact that this love never ceased. The apostle Paul argued forcefully that any walls between Jews and Gentiles had been torn down because of Jesus' death on the cross. God had acted in Jesus Christ for the Jews *and* for the world. The most significant and powerful act of God in history was the resurrection of Jesus Christ from the dead. Death was defeated and new life released around the globe. The resurrection was the ultimate expression of *chesed*.

As the Christian community journeyed on after the resurrection, they held firm to what the raising of Christ had accomplished for them, even when circumstances of daily life proved difficult. The book of Romans describes how the resurrection shored up their dreams during dark days.

We have peace with God through our Lord Jesus
Christ . . . we rejoice in our hope of sharing the glory of
God. More than that, we rejoice in our sufferings, knowing that suffering produces endurance, and endurance
produces character, and character produces hope, and
hope does not disappoint us (Rom. 5:1-5).

Paul maintained that our suffering can't compare with the
glory that will be revealed in believers through their promised
resurrection. He described the ultimate redemption as being of
such magnitude that the entire creation waited with groaning
and longing for the resurrected children of God (see Rom.
8:22-23). Paul described this hope as the basis for our salvation.
Of course, he doesn't mean that we are saved *by* hoping, but
that God's *chesed* through the risen Christ gives us every reason
for anticipation and expectation that can pull us through difficult times. "For in this hope we were saved . . ." Paul wrote.
"But if we hope for what we do not see, we wait for it with pa-
tience" (vv. 24-25).

Hope to Let Go

Bernice McShane was at home with her husband the night she
learned their son was using drugs. She didn't want to believe
it, but the evidence appeared inescapable. George had started
smoking marijuana and there were grounds to believe that
other chemicals were involved—his problem was spinning out
of control. Like a thousand other American families, the
McShanes were faced with a catastrophe.

As time went by, George became increasingly resistant to talking about the problem and his drug usage didn't abate. Bernice deeply loved her son, but nothing she said or did made any difference—George had wandered completely out of her reach.

Finally one night, Bernice knelt down by the side of her bed and prayed fervently for the boy. The agony in her heart poured out through her trembling words. After a while, she got into bed and thought about how to reach her son. He wasn't in the room, but Bernice could see him in her imagination, bent over a desk with his head in his hands and his long hair hanging down in his face. George always got upset after he was caught, but his remorse was only about being discovered.

Bernice could see him vividly in her mind and wanted to say something that could touch his hardened heart, but nothing came to mind. She felt hopeless.

Suddenly, out of nowhere and beyond her control, something extraordinary happened. Bernice continued to envision her son, but the picture radically changed: Jesus stepped into the scene and stood behind George. The risen Christ was in her meditation! Jesus looked over His shoulder at Bernice and said, "I will take care of this boy."

Bernice stared in astonishment, unable to grasp what she was seeing. As the picture faded, she lay in bed unable to speak. When she went to sleep that night, Bernice McShane had no idea how her son's problems would be resolved, but she had no doubt that his situation was no longer hopeless, and that it didn't depend on her. She let George go, into the care of Jesus.

George wound up behind bars, but the jail sentence was exactly what he needed. He kicked his drug habit cold turkey and came out a totally new man. As far as Bernice is concerned, the change has been a miracle. She can say, much like Paul in Romans 5, that she and her son were saved by hope, hope that was not an abstraction. Bernice is convinced that she saw the risen Christ and that it was His presence that brought healing.

Hope to Refocus

Joanie Brantley had a powerful relationship with Jesus Christ for many years. During many difficult times in her life, Joanie had known breakthroughs that kept her life oriented spiritually and her feet on the right path. However, she also periodically struggled with physical problems that didn't ever seem to get fixed. Some would come, some would go— but she couldn't find medical care to turn her overall health in a positive direction.

Joanie periodically discovered the Lord putting words in her mind. She always knew it was Him because what came out of her thinking during these times was never wrong. When Joanie made her own conjectures, she couldn't be sure about her choices, but when Christ spoke, the guidance was sound.

One morning, Joanie awoke overwhelmed by chronic fatigue. This seemingly incurable condition had pushed her to the end of her rope; despair settled inside her and she felt emotionally whipped. As she struggled to get ready for work, Joanie thought about the failure of the medical community to give her a diagnosis or treatment that would make a difference. Angry at everything she could both see and not see, Joanie threw an emotional fit that ended by her crying out, "I have no hope!"

The resurrection gives the
assurance that a heavenly Father
remains in control of the universe
and that we are not victims of fate.
We can count on the fact that
God will write the final chapter
of human history . . . and
of our own story.

Instantly, the inner voice of the risen Christ responded, "I am your hope."

Stunned, Joanie stopped and caught her breath. The message had been so unexpected and startling that she almost couldn't move. Four words had penetrated her despair and instantly changed everything. *I am your hope.* No longer was fatigue and exhaustion the issue—the question was whether or not she would trust the risen Christ to be her source of hope. Joanie found herself in a different place.

In the weeks that lay ahead, an auto-immune illness was identified and treated, but that good news paled in comparison to her reoriented life. Joanie had mistakenly put her total confidence in the medical world, but now her hope was elsewhere. She had been saved by hope.

Hope to Dream

Rather than the bleakness of a dark tomb, Easter morning offers an opportunity to look into the future with anticipation and confidence. More fundamentally, the resurrection gives the assurance that a heavenly Father remains in control of the universe and that we are not victims of fate. We can count on the fact that God will write the final chapter of human history . . . and of our own story.

In the meantime, we can see the problems we struggle with in a new light. Pain may actually prove to be our friend by warning us of dangers or the need for attention to troubled areas. Remember that pain produces endurance, resulting in stronger character. And an old Hebrew saying reminds us, "No matter how dark the tapestry God sends us, there are still a few threads of grace." God gives us grace to endure and hope in His promises for the future.

The hope imparted through the resurrection allows us to be dreamers. The God that cannot be seen empowers us to face that which might otherwise intimidate us. With this hope, believers can dream the impossible—and only those who dream the impossible will be able to achieve the incredible.

Notes
1. A. Schlatter, *Jochanan Ben Zakkai: der Zeitgenosse der Apostel* (1899).
2. Ibid., p. 73.
3. Robert L. Wise, *Crossing the Threshold of Eternity* (Ventura, CA: Regal, 2007).

Victory

Two perspectives emerged in the earliest days of the Church on why Jesus came and what He accomplished. In one view, Jesus perfectly followed and completed the will of His heavenly Father. He clearly stated, "For I have come down from heaven, not to do my own will, but the will of him who sent me" (John 6:38).

The bottom line: Through His obedience, Jesus brought life.

In the apostle John's first letter, he writes, "The reason the Son of God appeared was to destroy the works of the devil" (1 John 3:8). In the other view, Jesus came to defeat the evil one in all of his ways and works because the devil wielded the power of death. The death knell rose from the lips of Satan and no one escaped his terrifying summons.

In His crucifixion, however, Jesus engaged destruction to the bitter end—evil believed the grave had won. The devil thought the ominous toll continued forever, but Easter morning proved that Jesus had defeated death.

The ministry of Jesus can be defined by these two purposes: *fulfilling the will of God* and *defeating evil*. The resurrection was and is a critical part of this victory.

Despite this twofold understanding of what Jesus accomplished, today's Christian community sometimes focuses on the first purpose, that of accomplishing God's will. Certainly this aspect of Jesus' ministry offers us important clues for living. For example, the Sermon on the Mount begins with the Beatitudes, which define how God's plan is filled with surprises, reversals of what the world expects. The poor don't finish last and the persecuted can count on an extraordinary reward.

Often, we would rather focus on these promises than think about confronting evil.

We must remember, however, that confronting evil is how Jesus' ministry began. In the Gospels of Matthew, Mark and Luke, we read that the Holy Spirit led Jesus into the wilderness. After 40 days of fasting, He encountered the devil. In the midst of the struggle, the devil suggested that Jesus cast Himself down from the pinnacle of the Temple, where the angels would catch Him before He could be injured.

We've heard this story so many times that we might take it for granted, but let's think about it in a different light. I've stood on the edge of the present Temple Mount and looked straight down. It's quite possible that the precipice in A.D. 30 was even higher. A jump from it would be one quick way to kill yourself. It's a long drop to the rocks below. The Scripture makes it abundantly clear that Jesus was a human being, and nowhere else in the Bible do we find angels saving someone plunging to their death. I suggest that the evil one had the death of Jesus in mind from the beginning of His ministry. The crucifixion was the culmination of what evil planned in the beginning to take place on the edge the Temple.

This is not a book about evil that explains all the nuances and origins of Satan. However, we must not miss the fact that the people of the first century recognized evil as a major problem to contend with—and anyone with awareness and common sense recognizes nothing has changed during the last 2,000 years! Evil is still a big issue.

Evil Is Real

Spiritual warfare was not easy for me to explore because of my own personal confusion. When I went to college, I attended a liberal arts university that prided itself on living on the cutting edge of philosophical thought. In those days, the idea of a personal devil or a spiritual entity with personality was considered nonsense. Professors and students alike believed that evil was only the absence of good. When a sufficient amount of education and positive values are added to a bad situation, evil would disappear. What was needed, in their estimation, was more money to upgrade the cultural environment, a more comprehensive educational system to dispel the darkness of ignorance and an expansive system of enlightenment to eradicate the prejudices that cause misunderstanding. *Bingo!* The devil's dead.

At the time, this prescription seemed more than reasonable to me. I could forget those old Frankenstein and Dracula movies, and laugh at the caricature of a red-horned imp with goat legs. An evil-free future awaited the arrival of students who would make the world a good, just and beautiful utopia.

There was just one problem.

I had a sociology professor who assigned a comprehensive study on the causes of the Holocaust. Why did the Nazis kill six million Jews from 1940 to 1945? In gathering data for the

The death of Jesus Christ

set us free from the bondage that

our own sin had brought on us.

The resurrection broke the lock

and set the human race free.

paper, I stumbled across some unexpected information: When the Third Reich began systematically exterminating Jews, Gypsies, and Christian ministers and priests who opposed Hitler—as well as many other groups, such as the mentally challenged—Germany was the most literate nation in the world and had the highest level of scientific achievement on the planet. Germany topped the charts when it came to producing an enlightened and highly educated citizenry. The Germans had done everything my professors advocated! How could the experiment have gone so incredibly wrong?

The most educated and endowed nation in the world committed murder on a scale never before recorded in human history. No one needed to tell me that I had missed an important piece of the puzzle. The dismissal of the devil as an anachronism had sounded sophisticated up against those medieval drawings of a creature with a tail and horns, but ignoring the reality of malevolent evil was just as silly. I had to conclude that the cleverest strategy the evil one ever devised was convincing the world that he didn't exist.

Since the demise of Nazism and fascism, we have lived with the heinous deeds of communism and been forced to recognize the hard-heartedness of *laissez faire* capitalism. The American government committed serious errors in Vietnam and is now debating the morality of the Iraq War. Terrorism is rife. Civil wars dot the landscape of impoverished and disease-ridden Africa. Corrupt politicians work the system to benefit themselves and their cronies.

One can get caught up in all the horror, or stand back to see if something more is going on.

The New Testament expresses seven basic ideas about who the enemy is. Each one is important to remember:

1. *Satan is the absolute antithesis of God.* Not equal in authority, power or capacity, he is the enemy of the Creator. When the kingdom of God was manifest in the ministry of Jesus, it was the opposite of what pleased the evil one.

2. *Satan is the prince of this world* and declares that he can cause kingdoms to rise and fall according to his dictates. In this world, he arrogates for himself the honor that belongs to God alone. Satan's dominion is control over fallen humanity.

3. *Fallen humanity is his sphere of influence.* Unredeemed people become his tools. It is the view of the New Testament that broken people cannot free themselves from his burden and control without the intervention of Christ.

4. *Satan has the primary goal of alienating humanity from God and bringing human destruction.* In this sense, the Evil One was a murderer from the beginning. His methods are lying and deception; he is the author of every harmful means of defeat.

5. *Legions of demons are under his control and are used to aid in the destruction of humanity.* The New Testament

records that Jesus assaulted the kingdom of evil by casting out demons. Today we are not sure how to talk about this subject, but the New Testament affirms that these creatures of evil are still at work in the world.

6. *Satan wields the power of death.* The Scripture affirms that one of the reasons for Jesus' mortal human nature was to finally destroy the devil who held the power of death.

7. *Behind all forms of magic and paganism stand demons and finally Satan himself.* What is viewed as merely primitive or cultural can contain and conceal the reality of evil. Over the years I have enjoyed traveling, working and studying in Mexico. The ancient cultures of the Olmec, Mayas and Aztec peoples always fascinated me. History reveals that the only things that the Spaniards brought to the New World were horses and gunpowder—the rest was already here. However, when one studies the religious practices of these ancient peoples, one can't help but be shocked. Some of these groups believed that the shedding of human blood was necessary to keep the sun shining. Regular human sacrifices were required to keep the lights burning in the sky. As a recommendation for their culture, lopping off human heads doesn't stack up on the positive side of the ledger. But it does fit the idea of evil using paganism for death and its own purposes.

Evil *Was* Routed and *Is* Relentless

When Jesus of Nazareth was taken to the cross, He was marched down streets that didn't hold many people. I've walked the streets of the old city in Jerusalem too often not to recognize that only a small crowd could push through the narrow lanes. It has been argued that Golgotha was the remnant of an old rock quarry with a stone hill in the center. Crosses were erected on the mound, and at best, only a handful of people could have stood watching around the skull-shaped hill.

Can something of such magnitude, which changed the course of human history, only be seen by a hair-thin slice of the human race?

Yes.

What counted wasn't the size of the audience, but the consequences of the event.

As the Church moved from the event itself to surrounding the resurrection with theological interpretations, the Church Fathers attempted to explain why the crucifixion and resurrection were so important. They noted that Jesus taught that "the Son of man also came not to be served but to serve, and to give his life as a ransom for many" (Matt. 20:28). When Paul began to write, he picked up on this theme of *ransom*. Recognizing the universal nature of human sinfulness, he argued that Jesus' crucifixion brought redemption because it was an "expiation by his blood, to be received by faith" (Rom. 3:25).

The death of Jesus Christ set us free from the bondage that our own sin had brought on us. We had imprisoned ourselves, but the first Christians knew we could not break out of jail on our own—someone held the keys to the door. But who was it that kept us in bondage?

Satan! The evil one!

The crucifixion and resurrection of Jesus broke the lock and set the human race free.

Building on Paul, men like Irenaeus (A.D. 115-200), Origen (A.D. 185-254) and Athanasius (A.D. 295-373) understood that we are enslaved by the power of death, held in the hands of the devil like a chain. While each of their ideas was expressed in differing ways, they explained that the death of Jesus on the cross and His subsequent resurrection was a triumph over evil that established the irrevocable victory of God. Like the Normandy invasion in World War II, the big battle had been fought and won. The rest of the operation was mopping up the enemy and liberating prisoners. In the same way, Easter morning defeated evil forever, even if it would take centuries to liberate all the captives.

Peter began his first letter by describing how all-encompassing the victory is:

By his great mercy we have been born anew to a living hope through the resurrection of Jesus Christ from the dead, to an inheritance which is imperishable, undefiled, and unfading (1 Pet. 1:3-4).

The resurrection had done this for believers! However, Peter ended his letter with this warning:

Be sober, be watchful. Your adversary the devil prowls around like a roaring lion, seeking some one to devour.

Resist him, stand firm in your faith, knowing that the same experience of suffering is required of your brotherhood throughout the world (1 Pet. 5:8-9).

The paradox is confounding: *The evil one is defeated; the evil one will try to kill you.* The ongoing history of humanity is lived out in a war that has already been decided but that is far from over. The victory of the resurrection unequivocally demonstrated the limits and vulnerability of evil, but the devil never gives up on his attacks on the human race. The war is won, but the battle isn't over—every generation must enter the struggle anew, but not without hope and assurance. How can we be so confident? Because Jesus Christ has been raised from the dead and we live with a hope that is as bright as it was on the first Easter morning.

Why would any entity, devil or not, continue such a fruitless task? The Scripture lays the "why" question aside because it is more interested in instructing us in how to live well in the midst of the war. The battlefields may change and the uniforms look different, but the struggle doesn't stop. The Scripture tells us how to be ready, to make sure that we endure and are not defeated. The resurrection story paints a powerful picture that offers us the confidence and tools to stand until the end.

Let's examine the apostle Paul's instructions for how to stand:

Finally, be strong in the Lord and in the strength of his might. Put on the whole armor of God, that you may be able to stand against the wiles of the devil. For we are

The war is won, but the battle

isn't over—every generation must

enter the struggle anew, but not

without hope and assurance.

How can we be so confident?

Because Jesus Christ has been raised

from the dead and we live with a

hope that is as bright as it was

on the first Easter morning.

not contending against flesh and blood, but against the principalities, against the powers, against the world rulers of this present darkness, against the spiritual hosts of wickedness in the heavenly places. Therefore take the whole armor of God that you may be able to withstand in the evil day, and having done all, to stand (Eph. 6:10-13).

Paul continued with a description of the protection of God, but for the moment let's consider what his letter to the Ephesians tells us about our enemy: The adversary's persistence is staggering. Evil lurks in both the highest and lowest places. Deception hides in the corridors of power and in the shadows of your backyard. The worst of crimes can be perpetuated by the most brilliant of minds.

Further, we must change our perspective because we battle what can't be seen with the eyes. No flesh and blood in this fray. Our invisible enemy—our *adversary*—breaks into our visible world with tangible results.

An adversary (from the Greek *avtidkos*) implies an opponent in a lawsuit, an opposing attorney with a big mouth who appears in court as our prime accuser. In the apostle John's book of Revelation, the evil one is described as the "accuser of the brethren who attacks the believers night and day" (12:10). The roaring lion is not so much a beast ready to eat you up as he is a violent attorney who attacks relentlessly, shredding the witnesses and forcing them into confessions that are not true. For example, the hurting person may say, "I guess I'm nothing but a failure." Satan has won, even though it's not true. He is confusing, assaulting and violent in his intent.

Victory by Reversal

Satan is constantly working to produce guilt and accusation that keeps believers on trial. His voice echoes in assaults like, "You're not good enough! Work harder!" or "You'll never measure up!" or "You're worthless." Ever have one of these jabs slip out of your unconscious mind and leave you in a disoriented heap? Ever wonder where such ideas come from? Wonder no more! The accusations arise from evil, aiming at our areas of vulnerability. Whether or not there is even a glimmer of truth to the charges is beside the point; the emotional and mental assaults come simply because we're the target. It's how evil operates.

With this problem in mind, the Early Church learned something important from the resurrection. They remembered that it was when Jesus appeared to be overcome by death that He was just getting started. In the darkness of night, defeat was turned into victory—and the same reversal can happen when the adversary puts believers on trial. The intended loss can become unexpected gain. Peter's advice was, "And after you suffered a little while, the God of all grace who has called you to his eternal glory in Christ, will himself restore, establish, and strengthen you" (1 Pet. 5:10).

Like metal tested by fire, what was meant to ruin only makes us stronger. The adversary plans disaster, but from the eternal point of view, the risen Christ uses the heat of the trial to produce pure gold.

And how do we get ready to face the struggles? Peter believed that we must humble ourselves and develop an attitude of humility.

Where did Peter get such an idea? Remember where the apostle was on the night Jesus was betrayed? Clothed in cowardly arrogance and trying to save himself, Peter declared that he didn't even know who Jesus was.

In contrast, the Savior of humanity said nothing to His captors, and looked at Peter with one glance that must have cut the disciple's soul in half. The manner in which Jesus faced abandonment, scourging and finally death painted a picture of humility Peter had never seen before. In later reflection, Peter and the other Apostles realized that Jesus was the ultimate example of humility. The downfall of Satan began in the self-emptying of Jesus.

Humility is the discovery of our limits and the recognition that we must have help and assistance from God if we are to be sustained. The ultimate issue is not the pain that we experience, but our endurance. Humility keeps us from not falling into despair during difficult times because our source of strength is not ourselves, but God. In that sense, Christ's humility must have been a shock to the evil one, who would have concluded that Jesus' dying on the cross meant His defeat. In fact, it was the prelude to His ultimate and final victory.

In this same spirit, another of the gifts the resurrection imparted to believers is a new awareness of their capacity to reverse what evil intends. As the earliest Christians observed how the resurrection defeated the plan of evil, they discovered that the same possibilities had been given to them. If they faced their problems in an honest and forthright manner, they could expect the same redemptive results.

Charlie and Diana Waters successfully worked in the government in Washington, DC, when they became Christians and started a new life. Just before her conversion, Diana had purchased an Audi Fox—which turned out to be a real lemon. After numerous repairs and considerable expense, the Waterses decided it was definitely time to get rid of the car. However, their new faith confronted them with a somewhat difficult decision: Should they be honest about this hunk of junk and tell the prospective buyer the full truth? Candor would probably kill the sale of the car. As they prayerfully thought the problem through, they came to the firm conclusion that they couldn't lie about their Audi's difficulties.

Confident that the rest was up to God, Diana asked Him to send the right buyer for the car. She asked for a customer who loved Audis so much that he or she would willingly spend the money to pay for frequent repairs. She ended her prayer by thanking God that He had empowered her and Charlie to handle the matter with integrity.

A short time later, a young woman responded to their ad in the paper. The daughter of a wealthy oilman, the young woman was delighted with the car. Charlie spent 45 minutes explaining all the Audi's problems and ended by telling her that he couldn't recommend the car to anyone. The young woman smiled and said that she knew Audis had lots of problems, but she wanted to buy this one anyway. To Charlie's further surprise, she offered to pay the exact amount Diana had paid for the car in the first place!

Because Charlie and Diana relied on their faith, a seemingly difficult situation was turned on its head. It was resurrection faith at work in a real reversal!

Victory Over Fear

Perhaps one of the most difficult aspects of dealing with evil is recognizing the subtlety with which it comes. More people are affected by seemingly innocent or unnoticed intrusions than are directly struck by a major assault. Here's an example.

Alice Madison's mother died when she was eight years old. Decades later, Alice's daughter, Mary, approached the same age and Alice began to worry that the same thing could happen to her, leaving Mary an orphan.

Alice had always lived with the fear that she would die young. Her worries about death began to build—she even avoided going on a vacation with her husband lest something happen to her and Mary be left motherless. Alice's apprehensions became a struggle for the entire family.

As the situation grew in severity, Alice signed up for a program at church about how to hear Jesus Christ speak. She studied the resurrection as it was used to teach people how to find victory over their harmful emotions. Alice believed these possibilities were true, but didn't know quite how to appropriate the promise. Still, she listened carefully and wondered how it could happen for her.

One morning, Alice was washing dishes when her fear of death overcame her. From out of nowhere, the anxiety built to a crescendo. Dropping her dish towel, she stepped back and cried out, "Oh, Lord . . . please!"

In her mind, Alice clearly heard the reply: "Did I not care for you?"

Alice froze. Jesus Christ had spoken to her and His message was true. During the years after her mother died, Alice's heavenly Father had covered, protected and loved her.

She knew in that moment that she could trust the Almighty to cover the fears that arose as unexpectedly as His voice had spoken to her. Eventually Alice would recognize that the evil one had been the source of her fear and dread. While Alice's fears certainly were related to her mother's death, the continuing destruction they had brought over the years exemplifies how evil operates: by taking a natural concern and turning it into a paramount problem that we can't overcome.

Alice's daughter Mary is a grown woman now, and Alice no longer fears her own death. She knows that the resurrected Christ won the victory over death once and for all.

Victory Over Despair

When people don't sense spiritual attack, they become even more vulnerable to it. This is exactly what happened when Carolyn Martin and Josie McClanahan worked with a woman named Susan who was struggling with major depressive episodes. The two women were part of our congregation's spiritual ministry to troubled people, and both of them knew a significant amount about depression. They recognized that Susan's difficult times didn't fit a usual pattern. Her attacks occurred out of the clear blue, more like assaults than an ongoing struggle with a psychological illness.

Like metal tested by fire, what was
meant to ruin only makes us stronger.
The adversary plans disaster, but from
the eternal point of view, the risen
Christ uses the heat of the trial
to produce pure gold.

Susan Jones had no sense of what was happening to her. She only knew that periodically a cloud seemed to descend and she would nearly break in half as her emotions ran out of control. Her crying spells erupted like a volcano and left her disoriented and in shambles.

Carolyn and Josie worried about this young woman because during the episodes, she bordered on delusional, and her problem made it impossible for Susan to hold a job. Often an attack would come during an interview and ruin her chances of employment.

As Carolyn and Josie considered the problem carefully, they came to the conclusion that Susan had for some reason become vulnerable to evil, and her problems came from this source. Even though Susan had no insight into her problem, Carolyn and Josie felt sure that they were onto an important approach to a resolution.

The two intercessors retreated to a quiet area and began fervently praying by themselves for Susan's depression. Their prayers noted the victory that the death and resurrection of Jesus Christ had won over the work of evil. The two women prayed that Susan would be lifted out of this problem just as Jesus was lifted out of the grave.

A week passed and Carolyn didn't hear from Susan, but before their weekly prayer time with her, she abruptly called and said she couldn't make it. She'd found a job with a nice salary and benefits! After a year of searching, she had finally landed a good job.

As Carolyn listened, she recognized a change in Susan's voice. She no longer sounded dull, sad and drained of energy.

Instead, her voice was animated and full of life. Susan reported that the depressive moods seemed to have just disappeared. The last time I checked with Carolyn and Josie, Susan's attacks hadn't returned and she was doing quite well.

The forces of evil were routed by the resurrection of Jesus Christ. While people in our age don't tend to look at Susan's problems in this light, the cause-and-effect result is clear. She had been under attack, and through prayer, relying on the power of the resurrection, the evil of despair was defeated.

Victory Over the System

The objective of evil has always been to skew our thinking. As long as he can keep our attention covered by layers of ignorance or superstition, the evil one is delighted for us to languish in darkness. A lack of insight and knowledge keeps all of us stumbling around in the night while evil enjoys anonymity.

Our minds are the number one target, and evil will try to use our thoughts and emotions to lead us into darkness. The book of James warns us about what happens when jealousy or ambition corrupts our thinking. The so-called "wisdom" of this world is "earthly, unspiritual, and devilish" (Jas. 3:15). During a moment of contention, our thoughts may feel powerful, but James warns us that embracing that kind of "wisdom" is certainly not of the Spirit.

When the Bible tells us that Satan is the prince of this world, it is reminding us that he uses images, spheres of influence and institutions—"principalities and powers"—to shape how we perceive things. The wisdom of this world says, "Everybody's doing it" and "It's all about me," a mentality that particularly grabs teenagers. (Before you pass judgment, however, notice that Mom reads her magazines to make sure she's in on the latest fashions for spring, and Dad spends more time on the golf course than he does with his kids.) When we buy into the system that surrounds us, we're buying into Satan's lies.

The resurrection of Jesus Christ assaulted the entire system, and we do not have to be ruled by it any longer. When we align our hearts and minds with the risen Lord, we can live as citizens of His kingdom and join in His victory over the evil one.

Connection

The Christian faith is not a collection of ideas, values or a worldview but a personal engagement with the reality of God. Relationship—*connection*—is the point.

In my younger years, I was part of collegiate debates about everything from evolution to pacifism, and I heard academic professors deliver long, demanding lectures on topics ranging from existentialism to logical positivism. I enjoyed the heated exchanges between those who held opposing philosophical positions, but at the end of the day I wanted to hang on to something that was real, enduring and more than someone's personal opinion, however logical and thought through.

If I was going to believe, I wanted the reality of a personal experience.

While some called this a "mystical approach," and the Methodists of John Wesley's day might have labeled it "enthusiasm," the nametags don't matter. How could I proclaim a belief if I hadn't experienced it as fact?

As time went on, many struggling people came to see me because they also needed something real and substantial to hang on to. When your life is sinking, you want a life preserver that will weather the storm and keep you afloat. Pipe dreams and aspirations won't do.

I couldn't give genuine solutions by spinning a good story. The help I offered to hurting people came out of the crucible of my own need and experience.

I had seen the Lord.

Meeting with Jesus

Living in a time of great cruelty and suffering, the first Christians knew the importance of a deep, inner certainty. Because the Jews were a conquered people, they understood that the times were too treacherous for playing games.

One of the early symbols of the Christian faith was an anchor, an image of safety and steadiness for any who were familiar with boats that sailed across the Mediterranean Sea. The anchor conveyed to the Christian community that Jesus Christ was the strength they needed during stormy days, that God held them securely just as the anchor kept a boat in the harbor.

During the early centuries, when they were the outcasts of society, the first Christians gathered together well before dawn to celebrate their faith. Often they met in catacombs, because locals weren't likely to be wandering around graves and the Christians could worship freely. In contrast to other citizens, the Christians didn't fear being alone in a cemetery—through death had come their assurance of eternal life. The resurrection of Jesus from the dead had given them the absolute conviction that they could walk through even the termination of their lives with no trepidation. As God had mysteriously brought them into the world, He would take them out of it again. That certainty guided them even during the days when emperors like

Nero or Trajan sought their deaths. The emperors Domitian and Caligula could murder and mock and exile believers, but they could not defeat their confidence. Christians had "seen the Lord."

But how, if they were living years after His death, resurrection and ascension, could early believers go on experiencing His presence so profoundly? We can find out through a careful reading of the Gospel of John.

The prologue proclaims that Jesus is the Word, the Light and the Life, and that whoever accepts Him becomes a child of God. The first miracle John tells us about is the wedding in Cana, when Jesus turned water into wine. We often overlook the fact that Jesus' ministry began with an incident involving the transformation of the substance of wine. I suggest that John wanted us to recognize that Jesus was pointing toward the Last Supper that is, Holy Communion.

Next, John offers a series of stories that demonstrates the extraordinary power and redemptive work of Jesus. Nicodemus discovered that he must be born again, and the woman at the well was offered living water (again, similar to Communion). The 5,000 were fed, and Jesus walked on water. How could even a casual reader not be astounded by the person of Jesus Christ?

In John 6:51-54, Jesus describes Himself as the bread of life:

I am the living bread which came down from heaven. If anyone eats of this bread, he will live forever; and the bread that I shall give is My flesh which I shall give for the life of the world . . . Most assuredly, I say to you, unless you eat the flesh of the Son of Man and drink

Like the earliest readers of John's Gospel, when we come to the service of Eucharist, we should expect everything that John promised: We should expect to encounter and connect with the risen Christ in the celebration of Communion.

His blood, you have no life in you. Whoever eats My
flesh and drinks My blood has eternal life, and I will
raise him up at the last day (*NKJV*).

While this comes early in the text of the Gospel, it is a
clear description of what is promised through participation
in Holy Communion.

John continues by recounting the confounding resurrection
of Lazarus. This unparalleled event appears to be the final turning point in Jesus' ministry. Immediately after Lazarus walked
out of the tomb, the Pharisees began planning to kill Jesus. The
Triumphal Entry followed and Holy Week began. The final
events of that week take up a large portion of John's Gospel and
describe at length what happened on the night when the Passover was transformed into a sacrament for believers. Like water
into wine, the Paschal Supper became Holy Communion.

When you look at the Gospel of John in this way, it almost
appears to be a catechism teaching the initiates what to anticipate and how to participate in worship. Like the earliest readers of John's Gospel, when we come to the service of Eucharist,
of Holy Communion, we should expect everything that John
promised: We should expect to encounter and connect with the
risen Christ in the celebration of Communion.

"In Remembrance of Me"

Many evangelicals would be stopped short by such a suggestion.
An equal number of charismatics would probably also be surprised. Mainline denominations often perform Communion as

if it were a vestige of the past, and would be shocked at the notion. Nevertheless, if we go back and trace the development of the Church through 20 centuries, we find that Holy Communion has been the primary way people have experienced Him. Has this been true for everyone who came to the Table and knelt to receive? No, but throughout history, the Eucharist has reliably offered Christ's presence to those who seek Him.

Many believers believe that coming to the Table "in remembrance of Me" is a mental exercise—that they are to call to mind the fact that Jesus died for their sins. But this narrow understanding misses the Jewish context for what Jesus said and did. In the Jewish framework, remembrance is not *recalling* as much as it is *experiencing the event*. We can get the idea if we remember what happens in a dramatic presentation. If the play is done well, we forget where we are and are swept up in the dialogue. We become an invisible participant in the action.

For example, *Man of La Mancha* remains one of my all-time favorite theatrical experiences. Every time I see the play, I get lost in the music and the struggle of the characters. In fact, the first time I saw it, I forgot where I was. At the end, when Dulcinea sang, "To dream the impossible dream, to fight the unbeatable foe, to bear with unbearable sorrow . . ." to the ailing Don Quixote, I wanted to stand up and shout, "Yes!" I nearly got out of my seat. I was experiencing the drama in the Jewish way of remembrance. I was there; it was happening to me at that very moment.

This is what the New Testament means by "remembering." We are to sit at the table with the risen Christ and, as we receive the elements, receive Him anew into our lives. Just as it was on the night of the Last Supper with the Apostles, so too it is meant to be with us. The Christ is still here, waiting to meet us at the point of our need.

Nathan Monk's father was part of the Jesus Movement back in the '70s and appeared nationally with the Continental Singers. Eventually, the Monk family moved to Nashville so that Nathan's father could pursue his musical career.

As the years went by, Nathan drifted in and out of several churches, never settling into one faith community. In several of the fellowships, he encountered strife, disagreements and chaos. The net effect was to leave him highly disillusioned and disgusted with the Church.

Nathan's parents went through their own personal turmoil, which only added to his struggles. Later, he found a young woman he thought he loved, but his family opposed the idea of an engagement. The romance died like everything else in Nathan's life, and before long he found himself caught up in destructive behavior and thoughts of suicide. His inner world kept bouncing around like a rubber ball on a downhill slope.

In the midst of his confusion, Nathan Monk had a strange dream. In it, Nathan became a priest and the struggles in his life ended. When he awoke, the images didn't make any sense. He certainly didn't like Roman Catholics and brushed the priest idea aside. Yet the dream had touched a nerve that left him puzzled and uncertain. He began to suspect that a relationship with God needed to take center stage.

Trying to pull himself together, Nathan read the passage in the Bible that describes how Jesus sent the Apostles out to minister without money or provision. In response, Nathan sold everything he had and started walking from Pensacola, Florida, to Nashville, Tennessee. The long journey took a month and a half, but during his march, key ideas began to become clear.

Nathan started ministering to people he met along the way and doing what the Bible told him to do. He had read an article on clerical attire that prompted him to start wearing a clerical collar, and sitting in a park one day wearing it around his neck, Nathan was approached by an Arab named Abraham. As they talked about Nathan's attempts at ministry, Abraham gave him $20 and told him to buy food for the hungry, and if Nathan did it right, more funds would come in. Nathan rushed off and bought 18 hamburgers. When he returned, 18 men were waiting. The next week the same experience was repeated, but the number grew to 25. In a month and a half, Nathan was feeding 200 hungry people! Still wearing his clericals, Nathan had no sense of the reality of Christ but knew he was on the right road.

Through reading the Early Church Fathers and meeting with an Anglican bishop, he began to make sense out of liturgy, symbolism and Holy Communion. Slowly, everything began to make sense. Taking his cue from John 6, Nathan decided that when Jesus said, "I am the bread of life," He was talking about Holy Communion. His promise was that drinking the blood of Christ and eating the bread imparted life. Nathan realized that this expresses symbolically how Jesus is with us.

As he contemplated these things, Nathan realized that he had limited his beliefs about how Jesus is present in the world. He started to see that Jesus hadn't left us behind, but had multiplied the ways He could be present with us. This insight radically changed Nathan's perspective. Through Holy

Communion, he discovered that it was possible to be physically in Jesus' presence and to know Jesus was there.

As promised, Jesus made Himself known to Nathan Monk through the sacrament, and Nathan sensed His presence right there at the table with him. Today, Nathan is a minister and a priest with the Communion of Evangelical Episcopal Churches. His spiritual breakthrough came because he encountered the risen Christ in Holy Communion.

The Power of Symbols

Recently, a friend who pastors a non-denominational congregation expressed his frustration to me that the members of his church seemed apathetic about Holy Communion. The sacrament was functional, routine—something they should do periodically, but not an opportunity for spiritual breakthrough in the service. The pastor was disturbed because the congregation came away from Holy Communion with such little meaning and personal engagement.

After attending a few of the services, I suggested that two things might be the problem. First, the congregation obviously had no sense of the real presence of Christ in their midst. It was an idea they seemed never to have considered. "Remembrance" to them was no more than recalling Jesus' death and being glad that their sins were no more.

Second, I sensed that the congregation had no awareness of the power of symbols. A more significant sense of symbolism's power would have made a great deal of difference in their expectations.

Let me clarify by using a word picture. There is a world of difference between a stop sign and my wedding ring. When I come to a stop sign, I don't get out of the car, go over to hug the sign and let it know how meaningful it is to me to be standing there by the amazing little metal sign that makes big cars and trucks stop. Such an idea is silly, because a sign only has one meaning, and a stop sign's meaning is *Stop!* It doesn't represent a meaningful relationship between me and the sign, or between me and my car, or between my car and the other cars and trucks on the road. A stop sign is a *sign*, not a symbol.

A wedding ring, a symbol, is an entirely different matter. Every time I look at my ring, I remember hours of happiness and excitement lived with my wife over several decades. If my wife were to die before me, I would feel intense pain and sorrow at the sight of my ring, perhaps in addition to the memories of joy. Why? It's just a band of gold, after all. Because a ring is a *symbol*, loaded with unseen but very real layers of meaning.

Stop and consider how much of your life is filled with symbols. We sometimes buy automobiles because we want the model, the year, the chrome, the color, the expense to say something about us. We dress like business people, hippies, cowboys, athletes or supermodels because we want people to see us as a certain kind of person. Ministers in church wear robes and vestments so that the congregation will consider what they say in a light of authority. Our lives are loaded with symbols, even if we fail to stop and fully recognize what they mean.

Holy Communion is such a symbol. Behind the bread and the wine stands the unseen presence of Jesus Christ, waiting to make Himself known. Just as Nathan Monk discovered through John's Gospel that "I [Jesus] am the bread of life; he who comes to me shall not hunger, and he who believes in me shall never thirst" (John 6:35), you too can discover this as you approach Holy Communion with this revelation in your heart.

Connected to the Bread of Life

I stumbled onto the extraordinary power hidden in Holy Communion almost by accident. I always felt that worship should be alive with the unexpected to challenge the congregation to reach new spiritual heights, but it took some time until I decided that I needed to emphasize how receiving Holy Communion might open our eyes to the presence of Christ. At the time, we had many new visitors each week and the church had grown to a high level of community participation. One particular Sunday, I didn't know many of the visitors, but I decided to use a new approach to Holy Communion anyway.

"I want you to receive Jesus Christ," I explained, holding the cup and loaf in my hand. "Jesus promised that He'd be here. When you come forward and kneel, I want you to visually and spiritually ask Christ to come into your life. As you receive the bread and wine in your mouth, visualize that you are actually receiving the Lord Jesus. This is an opportunity to meet Him in a fresh and vivid way."

The membership started coming forward and I offered the elements, hoping that they might come to a new comprehension of Jesus' presence. The service seemed to go well, but I wasn't sure. I knew I'd have to wait and see if they made any comment.

Our lives are loaded with symbols,

even if we fail to stop and fully

recognize what they mean.

Holy Communion is such a symbol.

Behind the bread and the wine stands

the unseen presence of Jesus Christ,

waiting to make Himself known.

As soon as the service was over, I hurried to the backdoor as I always did to greet people as they left. Different people commented that something special happened to them during their time at the altar. A new reality had broken in.

Even more surprising, a visitor declared that he had met Jesus in Communion.

"Really?" I asked.

"Didn't you tell us that we could receive Jesus Christ while we took the bread and wine?" he said. "That's what I did."

I stared, almost unable to respond. I had gone out on a limb with no inkling that an outsider would come forward for Communion, but that's exactly what happened. And he experienced the reality of Jesus Christ.

Jesus promised life and He has never stopped giving it to those who draw near to receive. The next time you go to a Communion service, stop before you partake and pray that the risen Christ will reveal Himself to you. Don't dictate how Jesus should come; simply allow Him to meet you there in any way He chooses. The Lord Jesus enjoys connecting with His friends—and *you* are one of them.

CHAPTER 14

Confidence

This particular moment is not the best time for the Church. Attendance is down. Religious interest in America is on the downhill slide. Bookstores feature titles that applaud Gnosticism or that are based on the suggestion that Jesus and Mary Magdalene had children. Expressions of religious influence in government are in the minus column. Denominational gatherings may pass resolutions condemning war, deploring ecological disinterest by the government and a thousand other issues, but no one pays any attention to what they've said.

The bright lights of a national spiritual revival that flashed in the '60s and '70s with the emergence of the Jesus People and the charismatic movement are only a memory. The current religious preference in national life is pluralism (which the Old Testament prophets called idolatry). Nationally, we seem to have slipped into passive apathy when it comes to Christianity.

In contrast, extremists in the Muslim world are ready to go to war with the infidels (that's us) and kill them with a flash of the blade. All over the world, radical Islam is on the war path, willing even to commit suicide to kill those who don't call God Allah. Hamas, Hezbullah, al-Qaeda and a hundred other terrorist groups have their guns cocked.

Rev. Jerry Falwell's death was reported in the news with everything from appreciation for his political influence to condemnation of the Moral Majority. Ruth Graham passed away and Billy Graham is in bad health. The three major insurance companies that cover the majority of American Protestant Churches report at least 260 cases of sexual abuse committed by clergy each year on youth under the age of 18. The sexual scandals in the Roman Catholic priesthood are a disgrace that have rocked even Rome. Wearing a clerical collar in public is not necessarily a symbol of loving authority anymore—many people look at a minister with doubt and skepticism in their eyes.

What does it mean?

Nothing less than that it is time for the work of the kingdom of God to leap forward with new urgency and vitality! What better hour could there be for God to do a new thing in our midst? With pressing issues of such significant proportions, this hour is a great moment for the Christian community to recover its zeal and prepare for a great outpouring of the Holy Spirit.

The resurrection of Jesus Christ happened in an occupied country struggling under the harsh hands of Romans soldiers who could not have cared less about Jesus. God used the worst of times to accomplish the unexcelled best of results. The resurrection has not stopped imparting this same promise and power to those of us who will embrace it.

Really Tough Times

Consider what a truly difficult period in Church history looks like. Around A.D. 286, the Roman Emperor Maximian Caesar sent 6,600 soldiers north of the Alps to the city of Thebes. The assignment was to quash the rebellion of the Gauls. In order to make sure his orders were followed completely, a unit of Egyptian soldiers was brought up from the Nile. As it later became evident, all the troops were Coptic Christians.

When the commander, Maurice, and the Egyptian troops arrived near Thebes and prepared for battle, they found that the Gauls were also Christians. The Coptics also discovered the real reason for the rebellion: The Gauls had refused Maximian Caesar's order that he be worshiped as a god. They worshiped only one God, they said, who was fully revealed in Jesus Christ.

When General Maurice discovered the truth about the Christian Gauls, he knew they were his brothers in Christ. The 6,600 troops refused to attack fellow Christians. Maximian received Maurice's report, but refused to back down. His next order decreed that every tenth man who refused to fight should be put to death. Without any resistance, the soldiers willingly presented themselves for martyrdom.

When the result reached the ears of the emperor, Maximian was furious and ordered the decimation to continue until the soldiers yielded and agreed to fight. The response of the soldiers remained firm. Pledging their loyalty to Christ, they steadfastly refused to shed the blood of innocent people: "Christians we declare ourselves to be; we cannot persecute other Christians."[1]

Maximian Caesar's orders were carried out again until every last one of the 6,600 soldiers had been slaughtered. The soldiers simply laid down their weapons and offered themselves to their executioners.

It is time for the work of the

kingdom of God to leap forward

with new urgency and vitality!

This hour is a great moment for the

Christian community to recover its

zeal and prepare for a great

outpouring of the Holy Spirit.

Through their ordeal, Maurice constantly encouraged the men, reminding them of their commitment to Jesus Christ. Long after the executions were finished, the stories of extraordinary phenomena during the executions persisted. Fires meant for the victims wouldn't burn; shackles on prisoners were reported to have fallen off. Even after execution, some of the bodies were reported to have taken on a glow.[2]

Thirteen hundred years later, the great Spanish artist El Greco painted the "Theban Legion" to commemorate their brave deaths and the leadership of St. Maurice. The site of their martyrdom became the grounds for the building of the Abbey of Saint-Maurice where a continuous 24-hours-a-day prayer service has been held for over 1,500 years.

From the worst of times came the best of courage and centuries of spiritual outpouring. How is this possible?

These early Christians measured themselves only by their fidelity to the call of Jesus Christ. As the clouds got blacker, their steadfastness only became more determined. The ongoing witness of the resurrection had an enduring affect on these believers.

Living Hope

Christians through the centuries have remained aware that they live in a time between the resurrection of Jesus Christ and the ultimate coming of the kingdom of God. Regardless what happens in the world, they are part of a future that has already begun—though it is not yet fulfilled. What they do each day is part of that coming fulfillment. Therefore, they can be bold and assured even if their lives are taken. More than the stories of God's faithfulness in the past and promises about the coming triumph of His purposes, the resurrection of Jesus Christ has given them boundless assurance for the present moment.

No one expressed this more clearly than the apostle Peter:

> By [God's] great mercy we have been born anew to a living hope through the resurrection of Jesus Christ from the dead. And to an inheritance which is imperishable, undefiled, and unfading, kept in heaven for you, who by God's power are guarded through faith for a salvation ready to be revealed in the last time. In this you rejoice, though now for a little while you may have to suffer various trials, so that the genuineness of your faith, more precious than gold which though perishable is tested by fire, may redound to praise and glory and honor at the revelation of Jesus Christ (1 Pet. 1:3-7).

The Theban Legion understood well that they already possessed the inheritance Peter described, an inheritance that could not be corrupted even by an executioner's axe. As the years have gone by, the knowledge that struggles and difficulties are unavoidable has encouraged many believers. The pain that Jesus Christ experienced before His death cannot be compared with the glory revealed after the fact. As it was with Him, so it is with us.

In 1962, Larry Kalb was studying at the University of Texas and wrestling with a problem students everywhere have to face: What sort of career should he pursue? He desperately needed a job at the time. These issues can press a student to the limit, and Larry certainly felt the strain.

He stopped by a Baptist church because he had heard that there was a youth position open; he knew the job could take care of his financial need if the opportunity was still there. The conversation went well, and the pastor told him that he could spend the night in the church if he liked. Larry settled in for the night and began to think about the other problem that constantly absorbed his attention: Should he continue pursuing a future with music or was church ministry a better place for him?

As Larry prayed about the problem, there was a change. It wasn't like a surprise, but more of a logical follow-up to his need. The risen Christ was there in the room with him, prepared to help Larry in the struggle over what career he should choose. While his eyes didn't see anything, Larry's soul was filled with astonishment. The risen Christ was standing there, ready to help him work out his problem. Larry was so overwhelmed that he began to weep. The presence of Christ imparted comfort, assurance and profound encouragement.

When Larry speaks of this experience today, tears come to his eyes. But even more important, Larry is sure and confident that the risen Christ who visited him that night is still there. Yes—Larry Kalb became a minister!

The truth of Peter's assurances that the testing of our faith demonstrates the genuineness of our faith occasionally unfolds in surprising ways. Sometimes we are baffled when the struggle begins, but we must keep our eyes on the Lord, confident that the end results are His business.

Beth had grown up in the Roman Catholic Church, but discovered the fullness of the gospel in a Southern Baptist church.

Chapter 14

At the time, Beth's father was an alcoholic and she felt strongly that the answers to his problems could be found in the Christian faith. Yet when Beth tried to share her faith, her father, John, got up and left the room. His resistance seemed to be a testing of her newfound trust in God.

John eventually joined Alcoholics Anonymous and became not only sober but a vital Christian. John's faith radically changed his life, but in the spring of 1999, Beth's father died. Beth hardly had time to grieve before she had to prepare for the Holy Week events at her church—by this time, she was married and had become a minister.

After the Easter festivities came to an end, Rev. Beth Snare Owen lay down on the couch in her home and went to sleep, exhausted. An amazing dream followed.

Perhaps "dream" is the wrong word to use, because what happened was more of an experience, an epiphany. With her eyes closed, Beth could still hear her children talking, even as she felt herself ascending. Rising straight up, she felt herself go through the clouds. The sense of floating didn't frighten her— more than anything, she felt surprised.

As Beth came to a height far above the Earth, her father appeared and looked straight at her. To her astonishment, John looked younger than she did. She was 39, and he didn't look a day over 25, exuding vitality. He smiled, raised an eyebrow and communicated directly with her. "I am here," Beth's father said.

Hearing his voice, she remembered that it was two days after the celebration of the resurrection, and she understood what he was saying. Her father was communicating, "I am here in heaven. I am already a part of the resurrection believers will experience."

Beth woke up, gasping at what she had seen and heard. Knowing that her father was in some way a part of the resurrection profoundly encouraged her. She recalled the words of the apostle Paul, who said, "Just as we have borne the image of the man of dust, we shall also bear the image of the man of heaven" (1 Cor. 15:49).

Her father's participation in the resurrection of Jesus Christ imparted to him a renewed and refreshed personhood reshaped by the image of Christ working in him. John's resurrected body was imperishable, undefiled and unfading.

Comforting Trust

Growing up in the Roman Catholic Church, my wife's faith had always been a vital part of her life. But her mother's painful death with lung cancer was extremely hard for Margueritte to absorb. After a time, she came to a point of surrendering her faith and life to Jesus Christ. The spiritual experience set her on a new path that included discovering the inspiration and power of Scripture. The Bible became her guide.

I first met Margueritte when she came to the church I was pastoring. Sometime later, she told me of her feeling called into ministry and her interest in seminary. I began helping her prepare for that experience. As time went by, our relationship deepened and eventually we married.

Over time, I became more of a personal friend to my father-in-law. I greatly enjoyed Mitch Brantley, Sr., as a man of faith

From a Jerusalem graveyard, Jesus Christ

pioneered a new road into the future.

We have been invited to walk down that

path with confidence, assured of

His ultimate triumph and care. He can

be trusted to guide us through

whatever struggles lie ahead.

and character. When Mitch became ill, we were all deeply troubled. His death left the family stricken—Mitch was loved, a man worthy of the highest respect and honor.

In the months that followed Mitch's passing, Margueritte especially felt his death with a sharp keenness. Because she had so loved him, it was difficult to keep Mitch off her mind. She began to think about the times that she felt that she failed him. She remembered days when it felt like she had not been there for her father or had been insensitive. At some points, she felt that she had just been a jerk. As Margueritte replayed and lamented the past, she spiraled toward despair.

Finally one afternoon, she made her worries a matter of prayer. As she wept uncontrollably over her concerns, the unseen presence of the risen Christ drew near. His voice spoke to her and asked if she remembered the times when her dad had failed her. Margueritte stiffened, but the voice continued. Did she recall when her father had not been there for her or had been insensitive? How about the times that he'd just been a jerk? Did she remember each and every one?

"No," Margueritte answered. "I don't remember any of those times. "

"Then," the voice of Christ answered, "neither does your father."

For a long time, Margueritte sat stunned by what she had heard. Her grief had caused her to exaggerate shortcomings in her relationship with her father, but there was no reason to linger over her mistakes. Margueritte was forgiven for the times when she had failed. She could let go and truly go on with her life, confident that the risen Christ had reconciled and renewed both Mitch and herself. At that point, her complete recovery from grief began.

From a Jerusalem graveyard, Jesus Christ pioneered a new road into the future. We have been invited to walk down that path with confidence, assured of His ultimate triumph and care. He can be trusted to guide us through whatever struggles lie ahead.

Notes
1. John Crowder, *Miracle Workers, Reformers, and the New Mystics* (Shippensburg, PA: Destiny Image, 2006), p. 53.
2. Bishop Eucherius of Lyon, *The Passion of the Martyrs of Agaune* (fifth century).

PART FOUR

The Discovery
A.D. 2008

The pulsating lights of Las Vegas sent a thousand bright colors glaring up and down the Strip. The casinos and hotels poured multitudes of tourists into the streets beneath the gaudy, glittering neon signs urging them inside to gamble, watch the showgirls and have a few drinks.

Al Hart had checked into the Desert Inn earlier in the day. He flopped down on the hotel bed and bounced his hand slightly on the expensive bedspread—he loved the feel of the smooth silk. The air conditioner's coolness made the room perfect for what he had in mind. He'd been planning this no-restraints trip for a long time, and he was going to make the most of it. Unstopping a bottle of whiskey, he set it on the table next to the glass and then slid open the drawer on the bed stand. He wondered what a Vegas hotel might keep around the bedroom. To his surprise, Al saw a Bible.

Years had passed since he'd read a Bible. Pushing himself up in the bed, he opened the book and thumbed through it, stopping in the book of Romans. His gaze fell on the middle of the third chapter:

> Since all have sinned and fall short of the glory of God, they are justified by his grace as a gift, through the redemption which is in Christ Jesus, whom God put forward as an expiation by his blood, to be received by faith. This was to show God's righteousness, because in his divine forbearance he had passed over former sins (Rom. 3:23-25).

This was the last thing in the world he had expected to read in Las Vegas. Al read the verses again. He read them a third time, and though he wasn't sure why, he felt his eyes filling with tears. In contrast to the demanding neon lights blasting chaotic colors through the window, the Bible offered a peace that instantly invaded his thinking with a tranquility that he hadn't known in years.

Al would never have expected grace in the face of what he had planned to do.

Abruptly, Al Hart sensed someone in the room with him. He glanced at the Bible once more: "the redemption which is in Christ Jesus . . . an expiation by his blood . . . as a gift." The sense of a Presence grew. Al couldn't help feeling that the Lord Jesus Christ was standing there, saying the words to him. The thought both cut him to the quick and sent a charge of hope racing through him.

For a moment, Al closed his eyes tightly and breathed deeply. Nothing more needed to be said. He knew the Lord was by his bed. Intimately, personally, Jesus was there in the midst of that glamorous hellhole, offering him the alternative of untarnished joy.

"Thank You," Al mumbled. "Thank You. Thank You. Thank You."

The peace that descended permeated everything within him. Lasciviousness evaporated in the warmth of the presence of the Christ. He certainly didn't deserve such an intervention, but a wondrous love had found him. He resealed the bottle and pushed the whiskey away. He wouldn't be needing it any longer. Everything was different.

Al didn't know what to think, but his heart kept pounding. How could it be, in this temple to sensuality and sacrilege, that the risen Christ had stepped into his room and touched him with such kindness and acceptance? He guessed that must be the way the resurrected Christ works.

Grace.

Just pure grace.

What Next?

Is it possible for you to meet the risen Christ? The answer is emphatically *yes*. However, the encounter is not something you can demand or design. When experiences with Jesus occur, they are often an unexpected gift and exceed our ability to direct. Many devout Christians spend their entire lives in devotion and never have such an experience. That certainly doesn't mean there is anything wrong with their faith or sincerity. In fact, it is often a sign that no one has told them that it is possible to seek the face of Christ, and they have never considered the possibility.

I have talked with many, many people about their spiritual journeys, and I have noticed that the ministries of God generally come only by invitation. Our heavenly Father is the perfect guest, a guest who does not intrude until invited in. We set the stage by extending a request for Him to come into our lives. Without that personal invitation, the Lord Jesus Christ waits. It is not that the Holy Spirit is not working within us or around us, but the personal discovery, the encounter, the relationship, begins when *we* ask for and seek it. Jesus said, "Behold, I stand at the door and knock; if any one hears my voice and opens the door, I will come in to him and eat with him, and he with me" (Rev. 3:20).

The point is clear: You have to ask.

Actually, this principle is also revealed in one of the earliest accounts of the resurrection. In the tenth chapter of Acts, we read that Peter was in Caesarea at the house of Cornelius, a centurion. The apostle had arrived at the Gentile's home after struggling to understand how Gentiles could relate to the new faith exploding beyond Israel across the world. Peter said, "We are witnesses to all that [Jesus] did both in the country of the Jews and in Jerusalem. They put him to death by hanging him on a tree; but God raised him on the third day and *made him manifest; not to all the people* but to us who were chosen by God as witnesses" (vv. 39-41, emphasis added). Jesus no longer appears to everyone, as He would have when walking down the streets of Jerusalem. The eyes of faith are now part of the equation. Yes, the Apostles saw Him with their physical eyes, but Jesus appeared in response to their choice to believe. One must choose to have an open heart.

We too must make that choice.

My Choice

After graduating from college with a thoroughly agnostic point of view, I became a social worker, placed in a state training school to help teenage delinquents, unwed mothers and troubled children. During college, my reading of the works of Sartre, Camus and other existentialist writers had pushed me toward the edge of despair. I knew what the loneliness of life could be like. It seemed clear to me that the world was void of any divine presence.

In that frame of mind, I met a house painter who had left behind a good job with the State Department to be closer to his college kids. He wanted to share the Christian story with them. I was so amazed that anyone could make such a sacrifice that I listened to his passionate testimony about a resurrection I didn't believe in.

I knew one of us was crazy and assumed it was him. In time, I decided. I was the one with a few loose bolts.

One night in a men's prayer meeting, I chose to ask Jesus Christ to enter my life. When I left that night, I knew beyond any doubt that there was a God and that He had happened to me. It didn't take me long to realize that I was on an entirely new spiritual journey. Along the way, I joined a Methodist church and began working with a youth group. The congregation offered me the job of associate pastor and I started to work even before I went to seminary. The time was a great adventure.

One Sunday evening during the late fall, a minister named Dr. Byron Deshler came for a special meeting. As Rev. Deshler spoke, I was deeply touched and wanted to give everything I had in me to Jesus Christ. I came forward and knelt at the altar rail, offering what I was and might ever be to Jesus. With heartfelt devotion, I asked Him to come into my life in a new and deeper way than I had known before. The prayer time was intense, and I knew that I was making a highly significant connection with the heart of God. When I arose from this extended prayer, I returned to my seat knowing something important had occurred.

Immediately following the service, I left with a group of ministers to spend the night at Methodist Canyon Camp to help the next day to prepare a program for the coming summer camp that youth would attend. We unrolled our sleeping bags in a rustic cabin, and the night was so cold that I burrowed down in the thick sleeping bag. There was no heat in the building.

Although in deep sleep, I began to be aware that someone had entered the cabin. Because it was so cold, I didn't want to look out of the top of my sleeping bag, but somewhere within me I realized this person was very important. I was somewhere between waking and dreaming, and the moment had a hazy quality. Abruptly, a voice broke through my reverie and clearly said "Get up."

From deep inside, I knew this was a divine moment and it was far more than just a dream. At the same time, I was quite aware how cold it was and I didn't want to get up in such frigid weather. Again the voice spoke, "Get up and come out."

My mind wrestled with the command. Could I really get up and respond to the call of God when the temperature was so low? On the other hand, if God was calling me, it was crazy to keep lying there curled up in a ball!

Slowly I woke and realized it was nonsense to delay. I swung my legs out of the sleeping bag and placed my bare feet on the cold cement. In that instant, I was fully awake. For the first time, I saw the brilliant light shining in the doorway. A figure stood in the extraordinary warm glow—I knew He was Jesus Christ.

"Get up and come out from among them," Jesus said. "Touch not the unclean thing and I will give you a special place that I will create for you."

The experience was so electric, and I was completely and totally overwhelmed. As I stared at the door, the glow diminished and disappeared. I almost couldn't breathe because the intensity was so great. Without any idea what was going on, I knew I had to get out of that building and away from the other men, all of whom were sound asleep. There wasn't anything wrong with them; I just couldn't stand to be around people. Putting on a heavy coat, I walked through the thick trees and spent the next four hours trying to digest what had occurred. The experience was so godly, so set-apart, so divine, that I couldn't be around anyone. The only way I could go forward was to spend time in seclusion.

When I returned at noon for lunch, the men asked where I'd been, but I brushed them off. I knew I couldn't talk about the experience without weeping. As the years have gone by, the epiphany has become a guiding light for me. Regardless what I did or didn't understand, I know that I met the risen Christ. I can say with profound sincerity, "I have seen the Lord."

My point?

This experience followed my earnest plea for an encounter with Jesus Christ. When I invited Him to come, Jesus came.

Your Choice

I want to make sure you understand that you can't measure yourself by the experiences of anyone whose story appears in this book. You are unique, handmade by God, and you must let your distinctiveness shine. The point of these stories is not to provide a measuring stick, but a prod. The events are intended to send you in search of a deeper, more intimate experience of Jesus Christ.

Earlier in this book, we talked about how important it is to understand both the death *and* resurrection of Jesus Christ if

It is important to understand both
the death and resurrection of Jesus Christ
if we are to fully understand the
Christian story. It is even truer if we are
to experience Jesus Christ personally.
As one walks through the events surrounding
Jesus' death, one is better prepared to
encounter the resurrected Lord.

we are to fully understand the Christian story. It is even truer if we are to experience Jesus Christ personally. As one walks through the events surrounding Jesus' death, one is better prepared to encounter the resurrected Lord. I'm going to suggest what may be a new spiritual practice for you, but it can be an important tool for your spiritual growth.

Most of us tend toward either extroverted or introverted personalities. Extroverts are affected more by external sources of stimulation such as crowds, parties, dancing and other events that impact them from the outside. Introverts, on the other hand, are often quieter types that find themselves invigorated more by quiet, reflective events such as readings, art galleries or times of meditation. They avoid the noise of loud parties and are far more moved by contemplation or reflection.

Nothing's wrong with either group; it's simply one of the ways people differ. However, introverts often discover the power of imagination before their extroverted friends. Quite different than fantasy, imagination empowers us to emotionally experience events as if they were happening to us in that moment. While extroverts might not be as prone to use imagination, they can learn how to appropriate the power. It can offer them important breakthroughs—this is particularly true for their spiritual lives.

The Church learned long ago that one can use imagination to experience the events recorded in the New Testament and to make the same spiritual discoveries made by people in those stories. The imagination has a way of harnessing us to what once occurred in such a way that we can discover the same insights and passions that apostolic people uncovered.

In order to help people understand what took place through the death of Jesus, the Church long ago developed an exercise that allows believers to stand in the crowd as Jesus walks by with the cross on His back. Called "The Way of the Cross" or "The Stations of the Cross," these meditations have proved to be a significant encouragement for multitudes of people across many centuries. I offer them to you in an abbreviated form that can help you to accompany the Lord on His journey to His death.

The Stations of the Cross are used regularly in the Anglican and Roman Catholic Churches, as well as with other Protestant groups. They begin with Jesus' condemnation to death and end with Jesus' being laid in the tomb, and include 14 stations where each aspect of the crucifixion is considered. Along the way, participants think not only about what happened to Jesus, but also about what it means for them personally. As they walk beside Jesus Christ, they think about themselves in light of what He suffered. For these reasons, the exercise can be powerful and can prepare believers to meet the living Christ.

To begin a walk with Jesus through His crucifixion, it helps to have images before us for each of the stations. Your church may have small booklets with pictures available. If not, a favorite picture that depicts the crucifixion can offer you a strong visual focus. The point is to do everything possible to focus your imagination on the event, and a strong visualization tool often helps.

Select a quiet place where you can't be disturbed for the entire meditation time. Have a Bible with you or a guide that contains the particular passages. Remember, the goal is not to *read* and *remember*; the objective is to *imagine* and *experience*.

While reading about the crucifixion is helpful, your aim is to enter into the event as if you were standing beside Jesus. To that end, I suggest that you read the biblical passages at least three times, then go back and slowly experience each event in your mind. Let yourself see the situation, smell it, hear it, touch it, feel it. Release whatever emotions you feel. At some points you may be surprised by the depth and strength of your feelings. It doesn't make any difference how strongly or weakly you feel—the objective is to allow these events to unfold. Don't condemn or judge yourself for what you sense. Simply allow it to happen.

With that in mind, let's begin our journey, walking step by step with Jesus Christ as He makes His way toward Golgotha.

The Stations of the Cross

Begin with a prayer that arises in your own heart. Tell the Lord Jesus Christ how you feel and what you'd like to know. Don't be afraid to express your reservations or doubts. Pour out what has built up inside of you. Be completely honest about your objectives and talk to Him like an old friend. Because He knows your heart even better than you do, Jesus can receive whatever you have to say. Start with a straightforward sharing of what is in your soul.

The First Station:
Jesus Is Condemned to Death

Start by affirming: "Because of Your holy cross, You have redeemed the world. We adore You, O Christ, and we praise You."

1. Read Mark 14:55-64 three times. After you have the verses clearly in mind, allow yourself to enter this scene and watch it happen. Feel the events unfold.

2. In light of what you are observing, look at your own life. Are there places where you are afraid to be faithful? Do you have hidden areas in your heart and mind that you have not yielded completely to Jesus? What areas in your life would make you run if an attack came?

3. End with a heart-felt prayer that is appropriate for what you are feeling.

The Second Station:
Jesus Carries His Cross

Start by affirming: "Because of Your holy cross, You have redeemed the world. We adore You, O Christ, and we praise You."

1. Read John 19:14-17 three times. After you have the verses in mind, enter this scene and watch it happen. Feel the events occur.

2. Recognize that Jesus still carries His cross through His persecuted brothers and sisters throughout the world. Consider why you might not feel the needs of these people and be as readily helpful to them as Jesus Himself would. Why are you hesitant to be emotionally present to the pain of others? What keeps you from standing close to need?

3. End with a prayer about what you are experiencing.

The Third Station:
Jesus Falls the First Time

Start by affirming: "Because of Your holy cross, You have redeemed the world. We adore You, O Christ, and we praise You."

1. Read John 15:18-20 three times. As you watch Jesus on the ground, think about His words from that passage, said long before the crucifixion. Look at Him lying on the ground and consider how the world hated Him and will hate us. Are you afraid of persecution? Do you retreat from people sometimes because you are afraid of attack?

2. We should fear nothing more than the loss of friendship with Christ. Do you? What is the hierarchy of values in your life? What do you esteem the most? Could you release those values for Him? Consider carefully what you should be willing to put to death in your own life.

3. Tell Jesus that you want to be willing to die to whatever creates distance from Him. Describe what it might be.

The Fourth Station:
Jesus Meets His Mother

Start by affirming: "Because of Your holy cross, You have redeemed the world. We adore You, O Christ, and we praise You."

1. Read John 19:25-27 three times. Put yourself next to this group of women. Look into His mother's eyes and see her pain. Consider her loss of her son. Think about the emptiness in her life. Feel with her the impending death of Jesus.

2. How do you or would you handle the loss of someone close to you? Could you go on if someone that you profoundly loved died? Do you love Jesus with such a passion? Why not?

3. In prayer, tell the heavenly Father about the limits of your feelings, and ask Him to expand your capabilities physically and spiritually.

The Fifth Station:
Simon of Cyrene Helps Jesus Carry His Cross

Start by affirming: "Because of Your holy cross, You have redeemed the world. We adore You, O Christ, and we praise You."

1. Read Mark 15:20-22 three times. Be a friend of Simon of Cyrene and walk alongside him as he observes Jesus being mocked. Stand with Simon when the Roman soldiers demand he carry the cross. Experience what it feels like to walk with them to Golgotha.

2. Do you ever shirk the responsibility of carrying your cross of your money? Of your time? Of your witness? Should you consider dying to these obstacles to total commitment? How do you avoid being with Jesus under difficult circumstances?

3. Pray fervently about your own reluctance to carry the cross of Christ.

The Sixth Station:
A Woman Wipes the Face of Jesus

Begin by affirming: "Because of Your holy cross, You have redeemed the world. We adore You, O Christ, and we praise You."

1. Read Matthew 25:37-40 three times. After you have considered this verse, let your imagination allow you to kneel down beside Jesus, lying on the ground. Look into His eyes and see the fullness of His pain. Perhaps you've never considered Jesus to be capable of such physical need. Look and see what you find. How will you react?

2. Consider how you respond to people in need. Yes, there are hypocrites out there who play on our sympathies and attempt to manipulate us for money. At the same time, people all around us are in need and difficulty. How do you respond, even when you believe they are responsible for their own trouble? Are you kind and respectful? Resentful and not helpful? What difference would it make if Jesus was present in their situation? As matter of fact, He is. What will you do differently in the future? Consider your options carefully.

3. Pray about what you find in your heart.

The Seventh Station:
Jesus Falls the Second Time

Once again affirm: "Because of Your holy cross, You have redeemed the world. We adore You, O Christ, and we praise You."

1. Read Isaiah 53:4-6 three times. Reflect on the fact that hundreds of years before Jesus came, the prophet Isaiah was moved by the Holy Spirit to anticipate exactly the pain and suffering the Messiah would experience. Be with Jesus at this moment of falling and consider what He must feel.

2. Have you ever fallen? Have you made mistakes that put you on the ground? How did you bear such pain? How did you react under these circumstances? Did you carry it well or fail to exhibit the dignity you find in Jesus Christ? Do you still carry with you the guilt and struggle of what others did to you, particularly when it was unfair or undeserved? In this moment, allow yourself to die to the past and release the struggles of yesterday.

3. Pray about your decisions.

The Eighth Station:
Jesus Meets the Women of Jerusalem

Affirm: "Because of Your holy cross, You have redeemed the world. We adore You, O Christ, and we praise You."

1. Read Luke 23:27-28 three times. With the women, listen to what Jesus says. Consider what it means.

2. Ponder why Jesus, in His dire state of need, would suggest that the women weep for themselves and their children. Could difficult days be ahead for them? For you? Could Jesus say the same thing to you about your future? How might you handle tragedy? What can you learn from what you discover about how Jesus met His death?

3. Pray about the need in your life and ask Jesus to help you find godly endurance and strength of character.

The Ninth Station:
Jesus Falls a Third Time

Affirm: "Because of Your holy cross, You have redeemed the world. We adore You, O Christ, and we praise You."

1. Read Psalm 118:25-28 three times. As you stand by Jesus, allow these words to give you insight into His heart. Watch Him and ponder how Scripture strengthened Him.

2. Have evildoers ever attacked you? Have you fallen because someone set a trap for you? Under such circumstances could you say, "My heart will not fear?" (Ps. 26:2-3). Could you tell the Lord that you will

walk in faithfulness regardless what happens? Bend down with Jesus and ask Him to show you how to transcend the terrible moments in your own life.

3. As you remember that Jesus gave all He had to give, pray for a new understanding of what it means to offer up your whole life.

The Tenth Station:
Jesus Is Stripped of His Clothes

Affirm: "We adore You, O Christ, and we praise You."

1. Read Matthew 27:34-35 three times. As you stand in the crowd watching the crucifixion, taste, smell and feel the scene. Allow your senses to be heightened by the sight. Watch the guards divide Jesus' clothing and allow yourself to encounter fully this moment in all of its horror.

2. Does this scene break your heart? Would you not feel the same terror in seeing any human being dragged through such humiliation? At the same time, does it make you want to run? Look carefully and realize that humans are capable of terrible deeds and consider whether you are any different. Would it be possible for you to hurt others? Examine yourself honestly, fully, and face your own limitations.

3. Pray about what you find, and ask Jesus to remove any barrier that might prove to be an obstacle in meeting Him.

The Eleventh Station:
Jesus Is Nailed to the Cross

Affirm: "We adore You, O Christ, and we praise You."

1. Read Luke 23:33-34 and John 19:18 three times. Contemplate and experience standing there while the Roman soldiers drive nails into Jesus' hands and feet. Watch as His final moments begin.

2. Jesus told us that we must accept crucifixion if are to find resurrection with Him. Is that possible? Can you allow yourself to go through pain and rejection in order to walk into new life with Him? Are you ready to walk through the worst in order to reach the best?

3. Pray about your reluctance and hesitations.

The Twelfth Station:
Jesus Dies on the Cross

Say: "Because of Your holy cross, You have redeemed the world. We adore You, O Christ, and we praise You."

1. Read Luke 23:44-46 and John 19:30b three times. Let the words of Jesus ring in your ears. Look up

and see the sun darken and the sky turn black. Feel the desolation when He says, "It is finished."

2. What would happen if it was all truly "finished"? What would you feel if all hope had died? How would you face the vacuum left by the death of Christ? Can you dare to look into absolute emptiness? As you stand beside Jesus' dead body, still hanging on the cross, what runs through your heart and mind?

3. Is it even possible to pray? What could you say?

The Thirteenth Station:
The Body of Jesus Is Taken Down from the Cross

Affirm: "We adore You, O Christ, and we praise You."

1. Read John 19:33-34,38 three times. Walk with Joseph of Arimathea through these final moments. Let yourself see the soldier thrust his sword into Jesus' side.

2. How often have you been defeated? When did defeat take you down to what felt like death? How is defeat like death? Walk again through these moments of emptiness, looking at the void in your life.

3. Ask the Lord Jesus to carry you through the places of death so that He might raise you up with Him.

The Fourteenth Station:
Jesus Is Laid in the Tomb

Affirm aloud: "We adore You, O Christ, and we praise You."

1. Read Matthew 27:59-60 three times.

2. The ultimate death is the demise of self-centeredness. As Jesus laid down everything, can you stand at the door of His tomb and do less? Can you hesitate to walk away still in charge of everything in your life? This is the moment to die to yourself.

3. Pray that you can release yourself in order to receive Jesus fully. Pray for self-surrender.

It Is Finished!

You have walked carefully and prayerfully with Jesus during His last hours and traveled with Him into death—*His* death and the demise of *your* preoccupation with yourself. Death is death. Once entered into, it always brings its own finality.

Now you are in a position to follow the risen Christ out of the grave! You are ready to walk with Him into newness of life. Our ultimate objective is an encounter with the risen Christ. Our goal is to encounter Him alive and filled with life. In order to do this, we are now going to walk with the Apostles as they journey forward from the empty tomb. We will walk "The Stations of the Resurrection" just as they did, trying to uncover the meaning behind His resurrection.

You may want to take a time-out before you do the next exercise. Catch your breath and let what you've experienced settle. However, don't wait too long—the goal is to be completely ready for an encounter with the Lord Jesus Christ.

Don't worry if your understanding is limited. Even after a lifetime of study, the greatest minds are still baffled by this most mysterious of events, the resurrection. Limitation is part of the human condition. Go ahead and reach out. Touch the hem of His garment. Bring your doubts, worries and uncertainties with you. The risen Christ is ready and waiting.

The Stations of the Resurrection

Just as you have done through the Stations of the Cross, your task is to re-enter each scene and emotionally experience the event as the first observers did. Be there. Place your feet where the first believers walked and stand beside them. Let the resurrection happen in your life.

Near the end of the exercise, you will need a little cup of wine (grape juice is fine) and a small piece of bread. Have these ready before you begin your walk through the resurrection, and keep them close by.

Begin with a heartfelt prayer, telling the Lord Jesus that you truly want to meet and know Him. Be open to the different ways He may make Himself known. Yes, He can and does manifest Himself in visions and even physical touch, but His presence can be experienced without that kind of tangible encounter. Let Him come as He wills.

The First Station:
The Women Discover the Empty Tomb

Affirm: "Come, Lord Jesus. You have risen!"

1. Read Mark 16:1-8 three times. Walk with the women to the tomb. Talk with them about their fears, pain and dismay. Experience with them fear at finding the tomb empty.

2. Look carefully at your own reservations about the resurrection. What has caused you to doubt? What keeps you from being able to totally accept what occurred? Don't be afraid or ashamed about being honest.

3. Tell the Lord Jesus Christ about your struggles. Lay before Him the doubts you carry. If you do not believe in Him, tell Jesus why you don't. Be honest. Ask Him to help you overcome every obstacle that blocks your eyes from seeing the truth.

The Second Station:
The Angel Rolls Away the Stone

Affirm: "Come, Lord Jesus. You have risen!"

1. Read Matthew 28:1-7 three times. Let yourself feel the earthquake and see the stone roll back. Let the dazzling splendor of light fill your eyes. Allow astonishment to spring forth within you.

2. Let yourself walk around inside the empty tomb. Walk into your fears and reservations, and let the light of heaven descend into your darkness. Realize

that over thousands of years, this story has touched countless men and women.

3. Tell the Lord Jesus about discovering these signs of power that accompanied the empty tomb. Let Him know that you are not afraid to once again experience such awesome signs of glory.

The Third Station:
The Angels Announce the Resurrection

Affirm: "Come, Lord Jesus. You have risen!"

1. Read Luke 24:1-9 three times. Imagine the angels in dazzling apparel. Look at them. Let yourself realize what a spectacular moment this is. Listen to their words and allow them to sink into your soul.

2. Think about how you have sought the living among the dead and how you have lost Christ because your mind was fixed on dead things such as money, status, security, appearance and the accumulation of wealth. Examine any of your values that have kept you from true life. What has kept you from setting your mind on the promises of Scripture?

3. Pray and ask that light fill your mind. Jesus came to people who sat in darkness. Ask Him to fill your whole being with His light.

The Fourth Station:
Mary Magdalene Meets the Risen Lord

Affirm: "Come, Lord Jesus. You have risen!"

1. Read John 20:11-18 three times. Stand beside Mary in the garden. Watch her weep and feel the pain of not knowing what they have done with Jesus' body. See the gardener. Go with her to seek his help. Feel the astonishing discovery that the man is Jesus Christ! Try to digest the words Jesus speaks to her.

2. Mary didn't know who Jesus was until He spoke her name. Everything turned when she heard Him call her. Jesus is calling our names. Sometimes He uses a name we don't expect, such as an adjective that expresses how He feels about us. Ask Him to speak your name. Let Him speak in your mind and confirm His love for you.

3. Pray about whatever is in your heart.

The Fifth Station:
Jesus Appears to the Disciples

Affirm: "Come, Lord Jesus. You have risen!"

1. Read John 20:19-22 three times. The disciples are terrified, sitting in a room with all doors locked.

Experience their surprise when Jesus suddenly appears. Let your imagination help you see Him. Watch Him move among the disciples.

2. Jesus breathed on the entire group and told them to receive the Holy Spirit. The experience prepared them for the days to come. Ask Him to breathe on you and give you the Holy Spirit.

3. As you breathe in and out, turn respiration into a spiritual encounter. Ask Jesus to breathe on you, and then literally practice breathing in the Holy Spirit. Ask the Spirit to fill you just as oxygen does each time you inhale. Ask the Holy Spirit to fill you during this prayer time.

The Sixth Station:
Jesus Appears on the Road to Emmaus

Affirm: "Come, Lord Jesus, come."

1. Read Luke 24:13-33 three times. Walk with Cleopas and his friend. Listen with them as a stranger on the road begins to explain the biblical context of the crucifixion of Jesus. Listen to the man's amazing words and allow new insights to fill your mind. Go with them inside the house and sit down at the table. Watch as the stranger blesses the bread and breaks it. Recognize who this Stranger truly is.

2. Jesus became known to them in the breaking of the bread, or Holy Communion. He is forever present to us in this sacrament. As you pick up the cup and bread, ask the risen Christ to reveal Himself to you. Ask Him to come into your life with the same reality that swallowing bread releases energy into your body. As you receive the bread and wine, receive Jesus Christ. Surrender yourself to His purposes and ask Him to live in your heart forever.

3. Pray until His reality fills you. Thank God and praise Him.

He Is Risen, Indeed!

During your reading of these pages, you have been invited to make your own discovery of the risen Christ. Jesus always has a unique way of making Himself known, and He may well do that with you. Your life is a journey on which He is taking you to the best. That place is always with Him!

Come, Lord Jesus,

You have risen!

What Can the Dying Teach the Living?

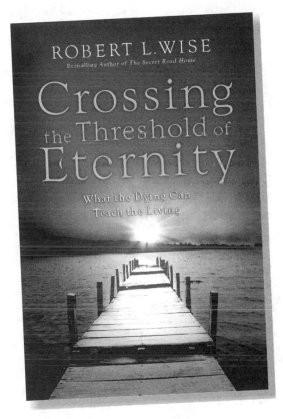

Crossing the Threshold of Eternity
What the Dying Can Teach the Living
Robert L. Wise
ISBN 978.08307.43704

If we listen and observe carefully, the dying can teach us important lessons that we need to learn in order to prepare for the end of our own life's journey. From standing at the bedside of the dying, Dr. Robert Wise came to to see important patterns and steps that the dying were tyring to describe—life lessons many of us miss when, because of our own fears of dying, we avoid having such conversations.

As Dr. Wise discovered, by stopping and listening to the dying, we can get beyond our morbid fears of death and come to a place of peaceful acceptance where we are able to look ahead to the end of our life's journey. The inspiring stories told in this book of those crossing the threshold of eternity can give us assurance, hope and a fesh expectation of what lies beyond the grave. We can all truly face our own mortality wihout fear.

More Great Resources
from Regal

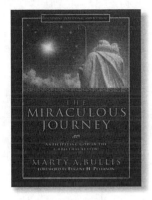
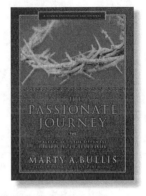
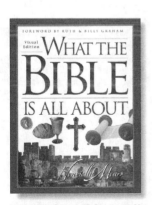
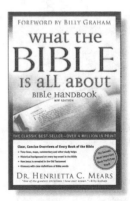